The Texas Hill Country

THE TEXAS HILL COUNTRY

A Food and Wine Lover's Paradise

Third Edition

by Terry Thompson-Anderson

Photography by Sandy Wilson

With a Foreword by Todd Staples
Commissioner, Texas Department of Agriculture

Shearer Publishing
Fredericksburg, Texas

Text copyright © 2008, 2010, 2011, and 2013
Terry Thompson-Anderson
Photographs copyright © 2008, 2010, 2011, and
2013 Sandy Wilson

Shearer Publishing
406 Post Oak Road
Fredericksburg, Texas 78624
Toll-free: 800-458-3808
Fax: 830-997-9752
www.shearerpub.com

Library of Congress Cataloging-in-Publication Data

Thompson-Anderson, Terry, 1946–
The Texas hill country : a food and wine lover's
paradise / by Terry Thompson-Anderson ; photography by Sandy Wilson ; with a foreword by Todd
Staples.
p. cm.
Includes index.
ISBN 978-0-940672-86-4
1. Restaurants—Texas—Directories.
2. Farms—Texas—Directories. 3. Cookery, Texas.
4. Cookery, American—Southwestern style. I. Title.
TX907.3.T4.T53 2008
647.95764—dc22

                                        2008019891

Information from Web sites of the businesses listed
in this book has been used with the permission of
their respective owners.

First Edition, 2008
Second Edition, 2010
Second Edition, Revised, 2011
Third Edition, 2013

                        10 9 8 7 6 5 4 3 2 1

Luckenbach Feed Lot photography on page 101 by
Robbyn Dodd
Noon Spoon photography on page 107 by John
Venable

Editor: Alison Tartt
Book Design: Barbara Jezek
Map Illustration by John Wilson

Production through Asia Pacific Offset
Printed in China

A Note to the Reader

This book is not meant to be comprehensive, but rather to provide a cross section of the food- and beverage-related businesses in the Texas Hill Country. We encourage you to visit and enjoy the many other venues the region has to offer!

The venues featured here are arranged by town, with the towns listed alphabetically. You can plan a trip of several days, visiting the many attractions found in several towns, or just single out a particular town to visit.

Although the entries are based on the most up-to-date information available and were verified prior to publication, Shearer Publishing does not guarantee or warrant the accuracy of any information in this product and will not be liable in any respect for any errors or omissions. We suggest that you contact the venue directly by phone or check its Web site before planning your trip.

Contents

Foreword

Because it serves as such a wonderful reminder of the value of sustainable agriculture practices, I invite you to enjoy Terry Thompson-Anderson's book, *The Texas Hill Country: A Food and Wine Lover's Paradise.*

At the Texas Department of Agriculture, we work hard to help those who rely on the fruits of the land: the peach, apple, olive, and pecan growers, the cheese and sausage producers, and the grape growers and winemakers. Texas offers an abundance of natural resources, and the Texas Hill Country in particular is a region rich with the treasures and rewards of plentiful agriculture. Top-notch products resulting from the tireless efforts of Texas producers are celebrated within these beautiful pages.

The food on our tables is so closely connected to the people and communities that surround us. This book introduces us to Hill Country farmers and growers who remain steadfast in their pioneering spirit and work ethic.

The landscape of the Texas Hill Country is an inspiring and breathtaking sight, from its sparkling, spring-fed, meandering creeks to its rugged terrain and rolling hills. Within the pages of this book you will see firsthand the true heart and soul of the region and all the resources it has to offer. You'll come face to face with the proud pioneering spirit for which hardworking Texans are known. Witness the contributions these Texans make on a daily basis, not only through their continued efforts to nourish our families with quality products, but also with their appreciation, dedication, and conservation of our beloved land.

Agriculture touches each of our lives and is a dynamic economic engine that powers our state's economy. Texas agriculture generates more than $85 billion throughout the Lone Star State, about 10 percent of the gross state product. In addition, agriculture provides a job for one out of every seven working Texans.

With the help of this book, discover the highlights that make the Texas Hill Country a national treasure. Savor the moments at appetizing area restaurants, bakeries, and herb farms. Visit award-winning wineries, tearooms, and apple orchards. Taste the rich delicacies of organic produce and perfectly aged cheese, and don't forget to take in the aroma of fresh Texas Hill Country flowers.

GO TEXAN and delight in the bounty of Texas agriculture. In Texas it's part of all of us.

Todd Staples
Commissioner, Texas Department of Agriculture

Introduction

The Texas Hill Country, a region encompassing all or part of eighteen counties in the geographical center of Texas, has been described as being somewhat like Jackson Pollock on a rampage. Fields of riotous color cover the countryside each spring when bluebonnets, Indian paintbrushes, and dozens of other wildflowers burst into bloom, announcing the end of winter in waving fields of many hues. Technicolor sunsets, glowing against brilliant cerulean skies, slip over purple-hued mountain ranges on the distant horizon. And speaking of horizons, we really have horizons—horizons that you can actually see in any direction.

The topography and venues of the Hill Country vary somewhat dramatically from region to region. The northwestern section has topography that ranges from the granite-strewn hills and spring-fed rivers around Llano to the fertile river-bottom pecan country of San Saba and Brady and acres of lush vineyards in the newly established grape-growing region around Mason. In the far northwestern reaches of the Hill Country around Menard the region is sparsely populated with a more pronounced look of only scattered vegetation and a rockier terrain. The area, known as the jumping-off point to the craggy Texas High Plains, contributed vastly to the westward expansion of the United States.

The northeastern region of the Hill Country includes some of the most popular recreational areas in the state. This is the part of the Hill Country where water sports abound on the chain of Highland Lakes, formed from the Colorado River, beginning with Lake Buchanan's headwaters at Tow (rhymes with "wow") and continuing through Inks Lake, Lake LBJ, Lake Marble Falls, and Lake Travis. The topography of the region is a mix of rolling hills in the eastern portion to craggy ranchland with huge granite outcroppings and limestone cliffs in the central and western portions. The land, however, is fertile, supporting an abundance of agricultural endeavors. Many scenic vistas of the limestone and granite cliffs can be seen best from vantage points on the water in the Highland Lakes.

Traveling through the fertile river-valley region of the southeastern Hill Country, the visitor finds a greater population density around New Braunfels and San Marcos, easing into smaller towns with a more laid-back ambiance like Wimberley and Driftwood. Heading west, you'll find Dripping Springs, often referred to as a "bedroom community of Austin," then on to Johnson City, Blanco, and Stonewall, towns with a definite feel of the old Texas cowboy life. The land is composed of rolling hills and vast stretches of open ranch and farm land. The area from Stonewall to Fredericksburg is home to one of the state's biggest agricultural endeavors, peach and blackberry farming.

The southwestern portion of the Hill Country, known as the Edwards Plateau region, was formed millions of years ago by the uplifting of a onetime seabed, creating a unique geology. The region is home to some of the oldest rocks in Texas. Part of the region, around Fredericksburg, is characterized by large granite outcroppings and domes, such as the popular tourist destination Enchanted Rock. It is a region of many springs, stony hills, and steep canyons. Oak and cedar trees are the predominant vegetation. This was a region of great challenge for the early settlers with its coarse-textured sandy soil, the result of granite weathering over thousands of years. In this section of the Hill Country the visitor finds the German-settled cities of Fredericksburg, Comfort, and Kerrville, which have retained a pronounced German flavor. Fredericksburg has several annual events celebrating its German heritage. Shopping and good restaurants are hallmarks of each of the cities. Between Kerrville and Bandera you'll find the sleepy little town of Medina tucked among gigantic oaks in close proximity to the meandering Medina River. In Medina you'll find an oasis of apple orchards. Bandera is cowboy country, home to dozens of working cattle, sheep, and goat ranches. Shopping in Bandera is an adventure in cowboy culture, yet the city boasts some thoroughly modern, upscale eateries. In the far western reaches of the southwestern Hill Country you'll find the quaint town of Leakey (pronounced LAY-key), located on the spring-fed Frio River and surrounded by deep canyons and hills with elevations of up 2,400 feet. Junction, originally founded in 1876, is known as "The Land of Living Waters" because there is more flowing water in the city and surrounding Kimble County than any other county in the state! The city today thrives as a shipping and marketing center for the county's wool, mohair, livestock, pecan, and grain production. The area around Junction is also known as one of the state's major deer-hunting areas, providing a winter economic windfall to many area businesses.

Those of us who are privileged to have stewardship of our little corners of this awe-inspiring region are fierce in our dedication to preserve both the unique culture and the land. The original pioneer settlers of our region and those who followed closely on their heels braved great odds just to get here, then they had to fight for the right to stay here, often suffering grave losses in the building of the Hill Country legacy. They were farmers and ranchers and sausage makers, bakers, brewers, and vintners. It's a place where the word "roots" means something, where finding fourth and fifth generations in our small towns is the rule rather than the exception.

We see our challenge today as having the wisdom to guide our small towns, those hidden treasures tucked among the hills, rivers, and lakes, in the inevitable switch from agricultural-based to tourist-based economies, balancing the tide of progress to allow room for both. To preserve and guide the entrepreneurial spirit established here by the pioneers. To welcome newcomers who have the potential to indelibly change our way of life, hoping that they will instead remain mindful of the reasons why they came here and help us to sustain that way of life.

The pioneer spirit is still very much alive in the Texas Hill Country. The newest group of pioneers to set down roots are the lavender growers. The willingness of the growers to face the possible hardships and the challenges of growing lavender in this region has changed the face of the community—both physically and economically through the landscape's aromatic and beautiful blossoms and the great increase in tourism.

Today there are more than fifteen lavender farms stretching from Fredericksburg to Johnson City, Blanco, and Wimberley. The city of Blanco, which calls itself the Lavender Capital of Texas, hosts an annual Lavender Festival the second weekend in June. The festival features tours of area lavender farms, each with special treats awaiting guests and cut-your-own lavender, speakers on a variety of lavender-related topics, and a Lavender Market on the grounds of Blanco's Courthouse Square. Lavender is becoming a big business.

The entrepreneurial spirit has also turned Mason County, with its slightly acidic Hickory Sands, into a prime region for growing wine grapes. The area has a unique microclimate with ideal daytime temperatures and strong breezes that help to prevent problems with fungus and mold on grapevines. The Hickory Sands Aquifer also provides an ample supply of good, clean water with a nearly neutral pH for irrigation. To protect the vines from damage by the hard spring freezes that plague the area, the ingenious growers of Mason County have devised a unique way to use a drip irrigation system to cover the vines with ice during a freeze. When the freeze is over and the ice thaws, the little buds grow on their merry way to becoming grapes.

So how are we doing in the Texas Hill Country? Well, pretty spectacular, we think! Hill Country folks are creating ways to turn that tourist-based economy into what is often referred to as "agricultural tourism." Visitors are coming to the Hill Country to follow the lavender trails, pick peaches and apples, buy fresh-pressed olive oil, and visit the wineries. In fact, the Hill Country was listed in a recent survey by Internet travel giant Orbitz as second only to the Napa Valley as an agricultural tourism destination!

Pick a road—any road, a county road, a ranch road. Some are paved, some aren't. Some are sectioned off by cattle guards, with vast expanses of unfenced land in between where livestock roams free. Some are bordered by ancient barbed-wire fences constructed with hand-cut cedar posts. Some meander past sprawling ranches with tall, deer-proof fencing and grand entryways fashioned from native stone and hand-wrought iron artwork. Chances are good that somewhere down that undulating ribbon of road, you'll come upon some remarkable Texas Hill Country food finds: a farm stand selling fresh, homegrown produce; a goat farmer selling hand-crafted goat cheeses; ranchers selling sausages made from game meats; a brewery producing fine beer in the European style of the region's founders; a winery creating world-class wines from grapes grown in Texas; honey processors selling honey from bees who feast on the region's largesse of richly hued wildflowers; peach orchards with roadside stands selling fresh peaches, peach ice cream, peach cobbler, and anything else that can be made from a peach; apple orchards where you can purchase many varieties of fresh apples, apple cider, and apple pies as big as washtubs.

Perhaps you'll find a berry farm where you can pick your own berries; pecan farms where thousands of towering pecan trees produce huge crops of delicious pecans each fall for sale in farm stores, where you might also find sinfully rich homemade pecan pies; fields of lavender in riotous purple bloom; the best barbecue anywhere, often served from roadside stands; free-roaming herds of Texas Longhorn cattle grazing on pesticide-free natural grasses; unique and often quirky cafés serving the kinds of foods Texans love—plate-size chicken-fried steaks with peppery cream gravy, cabrito (roasted or pit-cooked baby goat), and larger-than-life T-bone steaks. When the roads lead you to charming small Hill Country towns, you'll find an amazing array of restaurants—bakeries that beckon patrons bright and early each morning with the enticing aromas of freshly baked pastries and breads; decades-old diners, little changed by the passing of time, where locals gather for the daily specials; quaint tearooms, many of them doubling as gift and antique shops and serving delicious dainty salads, soups, and quiches that we girls love and the men we drag along tolerate; and fine dining establishments serving upscale foods with their roots in the region's rich heritage, in dining rooms decorated in the Hill Country style of understated, slightly rustic elegance.

Don't be surprised if you come upon a festival paying homage to a local crop, specialty food, or regional wines, or just the season! Maybe you'd like to brush up those culinary skills while enjoying the great Hill Country outdoors. That can happen—some of our Hill Country B&Bs, inns, and resort ranches along those winding roads offer cooking classes in conjunction with your stay.

The folks who call the Hill Country home are a special attraction themselves. Those from families who have been in the Hill Country for generations have roots that go back to the Texas war for independence against Mexico. But the region also has a strong siren's song that seems to be heard by the creative, entrepreneurial spirits who have burned out on corporate life in big cities. They come from all over to call the Hill Country home. They let their hair down. They let their hair grow. They trade in three-piece suits and spike heels for jeans and boots. They buy land and establish farms and vineyards, build wineries, open bakeries, restaurants, cooking schools, wine bars—you name it. The lure of the Hill Country is so strong that newcomers create niches for making a living in order to live here. The typical escapee to the Hill Country is well-educated and usually a bit on the eccentric side. But one thing they have in common is that they're a really friendly lot, the kind of folks who never met a stranger. So be prepared for some great conversations as you visit.

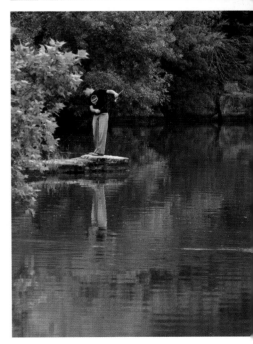

Welcome to the rich bounty of the Texas Hill Country, where there's something for every visitor. If this is your first visit, we bet it won't be your last one!

Diamond H Ranch

Bandera

The closing of the Diamond H Ranch in 2008 was a great loss not only to hunting enthusiasts who bought its live bobwhite quail to stock game ranches and train bird dogs but also to chefs who ordered its dressed Coturnix quail to serve in succulent restaurant dishes. In 2010 Chris Hughes, owner of Broken Arrow Ranch in Ingram, a purveyor of game meats, purchased the Diamond H Ranch and revived its operations as a quail farm. ✻ The Diamond H was founded in 1991 by Tom and Polly Harrington after they moved to Bandera to retire. Tom wasn't very good at retiring, and he was also an avid quail hunter who had noticed the declining quail population. Searching for a hobby to keep himself busy, he began raising bobwhite quail for hunting preserves and dog trainers. After selling 2,700 mature birds the first year, he increased production about 150 percent each year, working closely with the poultry science department at Texas A&M University and the Texas Agricultural Extension Service. The ranch was producing more than 30,000 quail a year when a poultry science professor at A&M introduced Tom to a heavier meat bird that he had bred from the Coturnix quail, also known as the Japanese quail. Almost a third larger than the bobwhite and quicker to develop, the Coturnix marked the start of Tom's gourmet quail business, which he continued until well into his eighties, when he decided to retire for good. ✻ Under Chris's direction the Diamond H Ranch will maintain extensive breeding, hatching, and brooder facilities as a state-inspected game bird processing plant. The quail are marketed under the name Bandera Quail, available as whole and semi-boneless birds, boneless breasts, and partially

boned quail legs. Chris is working to reestablish the brand in upscale markets, and chefs are thrilled to be able to serve the high-quality Diamond H quail again. The quail can be purchased online, by phone, through the Broken Arrow Ranch, or, if you're in the Bandera area, at the ranch itself.

1598 Highland Drive (off State Hwy. 16) • (830) 796-4540 •www.diamondhquail. com

BANDERA QUAIL WITH BACON, JALAPEÑO, AND CHEESE STUFFING

This recipe can also be prepared with whole, unboned quail or with quail breasts.

Yield: 4 servings

4 cups cubed (½-inch) French bread
6 slices applewood-smoked bacon, cut into ½-inch dice
1 large garlic clove, minced
1 small onion, cut into ¼-inch dice
3 jalapeños, seeded and minced
1 cup rich chicken broth
1 cup (4 ounces) shredded cheddar cheese
Salt and freshly ground black pepper to taste
8 Diamond H semi-boneless quail
Olive oil
Chili powder

Preheat oven to 400 degrees. Spread the bread cubes in a single layer on a baking sheet. Toast in preheated oven for 8 to 10 minutes, or until lightly browned. Set aside.

Cook the bacon in a heavy-bottomed 12-inch skillet over medium heat until browned but not completely crisp. Remove with a slotted spoon and drain on absorbent paper towels. Pour off all but 2 tablespoons of the bacon drippings. Heat the drippings and sauté the garlic, onion, and jalapeños until the onion is wilted and transparent, about 5 minutes. Add ¼ cup of the chicken broth, scraping up bits of browned bits from the bottom of the pan. Add the toasted bread cubes, stirring gently to blend. Add the remaining broth, ¼ cup at a time, until the bread is moist but not soggy. Remove skillet from heat and mix in the cheese. Season stuffing with salt and pepper.

Allow the stuffing to cool completely before stuffing the quail. (Thoroughly cooled stuffing helps prevent the formation of harmful bacteria.) Pat the quail dry with paper towels and fill each bird with a portion of the stuffing. Using a pastry brush, baste each quail with a little olive oil. Season on all sides with salt and pepper and a dash of the chili powder.

Heat a gas grill to medium-high. Place the quail on the grill, breast side down, and cook for about 4 minutes, or until the breast skin is browned and slightly crisp. Turn and cook an additional 3 to 4 minutes. Move the quail to the edge of the grill. Baste again with olive oil. Cook for 2 more minutes, basting and turning, or until the skin is crisp on all sides. Serve hot.

(Diamond H Ranch)

BANDERA

ROASTED POBLANO CAESAR SALAD WITH CORN BREAD CROUTONS

This fabulous salad is one of the most popular items on the Grotto menu. To break up the preparation, make the dressing one day and the croutons the next day—then simply put the salad together. The salad is hearty enough to serve as a luncheon entrée with some hot bread and a nice glass of chilled sauvignon blanc or viognier. The leftover dressing will keep in the refrigerator for about a week.

Yield: 6 to 8 servings

12 cups chopped romaine lettuce
Grated Cotija cheese
Chopped cilantro
Freshly squeezed lemon juice
Freshly cracked black pepper
Mexican chile-limón powder (equal parts lemon pepper and chili powder)
Corn Bread Croutons (see recipe below)

Dressing

2 tablespoons fresh lemon juice, plus a little more for finishing the salad
3 teaspoons anchovy paste
1½ teaspoons Worcestershire sauce
2 teaspoons minced garlic
1 teaspoon black pepper
1 tablespoon minced cilantro
½ cup chopped roasted poblano chilies
1½ teaspoons green curry paste (available in Asian markets)
1 quart real mayonnaise

Corn Bread Croutons

½ cup polenta or coarse cornmeal
1 cup buttermilk
1 tablespoon Texas wildflower honey
1 tablespoon melted butter
2 eggs
⅔ cup all-purpose flour
2 tablespoons sugar
2 tablespoons brown sugar
2¼ teaspoons baking powder
⅛ teaspoon baking soda
½ teaspoon kosher salt
10 slices applewood-smoked bacon, cooked until crisp, drained, and cut into tiny bits

(continued)

The Grotto Grill and Coffee Bar

Bandera

The Grotto Grill and Coffee Bar is one of Bandera's most pleasant surprises. Amid the city's cowboy culture, owner-chef Jason Boyd has created an inviting little space, which he describes as urban-retro-modern, and filled it with local art and tables that he designed and made himself. In fact, he even built the kitchen. ❁ Jason is a self-taught culinary master who acquired his passion for food from his mother, grandmother, and aunts, all marvelous cooks who had vegetable gardens. California chefs Thomas Keller of the French Laundry in Yountville and Alice Waters of Chez Panisse in Berkeley are his main culinary influences. He loves to make people happy with food, noting how much of our lives we spend together around a table sharing food and conversation. With the Grotto Grill, he wanted to create simple food in a casual atmosphere, as though you were a guest in his home. ❁ His food, made with local, organic, seasonal ingredients, is simple in nature but complex in taste. Eclectic wines are served as well as organic, fair-trade, shade-grown, bird-friendly coffees. Nine-five percent of everything available at the restaurant is made on the premises. ❁ The Grotto serves lunch from Tuesday through Saturday, brunch on Sundays, and dinner on Fridays and Saturdays. The lunch menu is loaded with all sort of tempting goodies from focaccia bread as well as hand-made pizzas with a fabulous crust and myriad toppings. There are pasta dishes, soups, meal-size salads, and a sandwich for every whim. The brunch menu offers a variety of egg dishes and even a good ol' fried egg sandwich. ❁ The dinner menus change weekly and feature reasonably priced dishes that would cost you a small fortune in the big city—Duck Soup with Wild Mushrooms, Chilean Sea Bass with Parsnips, Spinach & Saffron-Vanilla Sauce, to name just a few.

907 13th Street • (830) 796-9555

Make the dressing. Combine all ingredients in blender except the mayonnaise. Puree until smooth. Turn mixture out into a mixing bowl and whisk in the mayonnaise to make a smooth dressing. Adjust seasonings to taste. The dressing should have a fairly pronounced lemon and garlic balance, with just a hint of cilantro and a slight sting from the poblano chilies. Refrigerate until ready to use.

Make the Corn Bread Croutons. Preheat oven to 350 degrees. Grease a large baking sheet and set aside. Stir the polenta and buttermilk together in a large bowl. Whisk the honey and butter together, then add to the polenta. Add the eggs and beat to mix well; set aside.

In bowl of electric mixer combine the flour, sugar, brown sugar, baking powder, baking soda, and kosher salt. Add the buttermilk mixture and beat, starting at low speed and increasing speed as dry ingredients are moistened; mix until well blended. Turn mixture out into the baking sheet; form a very thin layer (about $5/8$ inch thick) and scatter the chopped bacon over the entire surface, pushing it into the polenta mixture. Bake in preheated oven for about 30 minutes, or until firm and just turning brown. Cool. Cut into crouton-size squares and turn out onto a clean baking sheet. Reduce oven heat to 300 degrees and bake for 20 to 30 minutes, or until dry and crisp. (Leave the oven door open so the moisture can escape and the croutons can dry out completely.) As the croutons brown, watch carefully and take care not overbrown them. Cool on a wire rack and store in an airtight container until ready to use.

To assemble the salad, toss the chopped romaine with the desired amount of dressing and Cotija cheese. Place a serving of the greens on each plate and garnish with the cilantro, lemon juice, black pepper, and Mexican chile-limón powder. Sprinkle with some of the Corn Bread Croutons and serve.

(The Grotto Grill and Coffee Bar)

Alamosa Wine Cellars

Bend

Winemaker Jim Johnson, who owns Alamosa Wine Cellars with his wife, Karen, has often been referred to as "the future of Texas wine." Anyone who has tasted his wines will surely agree. Jim has bucked the tide of tradition in Texas wines, always maintaining that Texas wineries should be growing those varietals that are adaptable to our hot climate. So he didn't plant cabernet or chardonnay or merlot, but rather Mediterranean varietals like tempranillo (from which he makes his award-wining El Guapo), sangiovese, syrah, chenin blanc (from which he crafts Jacque Lapin), and viognier (Alamosa's Viognier is one of the best in the state). After watching the success of Jim's wines, many other Texas wineries are slowly coming around to his way of thinking. He's uncovered the real niche for Texas wines with varietals from Italy's Tuscany, Spain's Rioja, and the Rhone Valley in France. ❧ After working many years in the "oil patch" in Houston, he packed up everything he owned and headed to California, where he graduated from the University of California's Davis campus with a degree in enology and viticulture. He hung around California for a few years, working at some pretty impressive wineries—such as Heitz Cellars and St. Francis—but Texas was home. ❧ Alamosa Wine Cellars is one of the most remote of the Hill Country wineries, located in the sparsely populated, scenic rolling hills west of Bend off Highway 580. The winery was built in 1999, just in time for the harvest that year. It was constructed only as a production facility because Texas law prohibited the retail sale of wine in "dry" jurisdictions at the time. ❧ After the law was changed in 2001, Jim and Karen set up a tasting bar for weekend tastings. In 2004 they expanded the winery to include more barrel storage and a spacious tasting room with a fireplace made of San Saba limestone, which is very inviting in the winter months. The retail space is furnished with antique fixtures from Karen's parents' mercantile store, its venerable counter serving as the tasting bar. The facility has a covered veranda, the perfect place for picnics or just enjoying a glass of wine while gazing out over the vineyard and hills. The Johnsons run the tasting room themselves, and you'll feel welcome from the minute you turn onto the lavender-lined road that leads to the winery.

**677 CR 430 (Bend) • (325) 628-3313 • www.alamosawinecellars.com •
Tasting Room & Gift Shop, 2201 U.S. 281 S., Palapas Springs Shopping
Center (Lampasas) • (512) 556-0001**

BEND

HERB-BAKED GOAT FETA CHEESE WITH GARLIC, KALAMATA OLIVES, AND ALMONDS

Yield: 4 to 6 servings as an appetizer

8 ounces CKC Farms Goat Feta cheese cubes
16 pitted kalamata olives
4 large garlic cloves, cut into thin slices
16 blanched whole almonds
1 cup olive oil
1 teaspoon minced fresh rosemary
1 tablespoon minced fresh parsley
1 teaspoon crushed red pepper flakes
1¼ teaspoons freshly ground black pepper
Salt to taste
French baguette, cut into 1-inch slices

Preheat oven to 425 degrees. Place the cheese in an oven-proof 8- to 10-inch oval au gratin dish. Scatter the olives, garlic, and almonds around the dish. Combine the olive oil, rosemary, parsley, red pepper, black pepper, and salt in a bowl; whisk to blend well and flavor the oil. Pour the oil mixture evenly over the cheese. Place dish in preheated oven and bake for about 10 minutes, or until the cheese is very lightly browned and the oil is bubbling. Let cool for about 6 minutes before serving. Serve with a basket of baguette slices for dipping and spreading.

(Terry Thompson-Anderson)

CKC Farms

Blanco

CKC Farms is one of the Hill Country's newest producers of fine-quality goat cheeses, all made by Chrissy Omo, who first learned the art of making goat cheese when she was barely fourteen and living with her family in Germany and Italy. ❦ Being an adventurous eater, she tried all the local cheeses but developed a great interest in the many styles of goat cheese she discovered. In Bologna, Italy, she would make prolonged visits to goat cheese producers, studying their various methods and asking hundreds of questions. The cheese makers were fascinated that one so young could have such a grand interest in making cheese, so she was welcomed by the masters and learned from them. ❦ When the family returned home to Blanco, with the encouragement of her mother, Adriana, Chrissy began to build her herd of Alpine, La Mancha, and Saaman goats while she was still in high school. Upon graduating, she began to market her cheeses to local farmer's markets. ❦ The cheeses are now available in many upscale markets in Austin and throughout the Hill Country, including McCall Creek Farms Market. Upscale restaurants clamor for allotments of her limited production. CKC Farms produces plain chèvre, a blue-veined goat cheese, goat feta cheese, and several flavored and seasonal blends. ❦ Hill Country cheese lovers eagerly await each new variety that Chrissy produces. In the spring of 2008 she released a sensational Romano cheese, which she perfected on a recent trip to Italy.

17505 FM 32 •
(830) 833-5669 •
www.ckcfarms.com

FISH TACOS

Yield: 2 tacos

3 tablespoons canola oil
1 (6-ounce) fresh fish fillet
Salt and freshly ground black pepper
1 tablespoon butter
1 garlic clove, minced
1 tablespoon minced flat-leaf parsley
1 teaspoon freshly squeezed lemon juice
2 corn tortillas
3 to 4 ounces shredded red cabbage
Chipotle aioli
Crumbled queso fresco cheese
Chopped cilantro
Thinly sliced onion

Heat the oil in a skillet. Salt and pepper the fish filet and sear it in the hot oil until golden brown on both sides. Add the butter, garlic, parsley, and lemon juice. Cook to lightly brown the butter. Remove from heat.

Heat the tortillas until they will bend without tearing. Layer the tacos with half of the fish mixture and the cabbage. Drizzle desired amount of chipotle aioli over the tacos, fold them in half, and garnish with the cheese, cilantro, and onion. Serve at once.

(Zocalo Eclectic Café)

Zocalo Eclectic Café

Blanco

Located on Pecan Street, one block east of Main, in a charming little house with a beckoning front porch and a roomy back deck, the café is named, appropriately, for the central plaza in Mexico City. The ambiance of the interior has been enhanced by a vivid palate of Mexican colors and local artwork. The eatery was opened in early 2011 by Rich Hopkins, a Fort Worth native and a noted musician who has recorded more than a dozen albums.

So how did a world-traveled performer wind up as the owner of a little café in Blanco? During a visit to the area, Rich and his partner and fiancée, Lisa Novak, stayed at a cabin on a beautiful stretch of the Blanco River and fell in love with the laid-back ways of the Hill Country. So why not invest in a lifelong dream of opening up a small café? They hired Bonnie Travis to manage the café and found an innovative young chef to head the kitchen. The team took the little café from a breakfast and lunch venue to a full-time restaurant with an impressive dinner menu as well as a Sunday brunch serving all the great classic brunch dishes, or just plain old eggs, bacon, and biscuits if you'd rather. Music will play a major role at the café, and Rich is building a beer garden and outdoor stage for concerts adjacent to the restaurant. The menu is eclectic, with offerings from around the globe. The selection runs the gamut from appetizers (even at lunch) to gourmet burgers served on ciabatta rolls, excellently crafted sandwiches, great salads, hot plates, daily specials, and fish tacos, one of the café's best sellers, plus a homemade pie and cake du jour. Produce is sourced from local farmers, and the wines and beers are also locally produced. Even the diners are eclectic, with a mix of local regulars, tourists, and lots of Austinites who make the drive to enjoy the café's good food and folksy, bohemian charm.

520 Pecan Street •
(830) 833-4300 •
www.zocaloblanco.com

4th Street Market
Blanco

First off, the market isn't on 4th Street—although it started out there in an old meat market where owner Lester Coldewey learned the craft of butchering. He eventually bought the meat market and, in due time, relocated it in a new, larger building across the river on Chandler Street (the continuation of 4th Street). He also moved the huge old meat scale from the original market. Lester and his wife, Carol, say that over the years customers would bring their children into the market and ask the butcher to weigh them on that big scale to "see how they're growing." ❄ The new market is a squeaky-clean, inviting space with a large meat case loaded with hand-cut roasts, steaks, chops, meat ground fresh daily, and tons of the sausage for which Lester is known far and wide, made from his secret formula. It's some of the best sausage you'll find anywhere! He makes some dynamite jerky and dry-cured sausages as well. The hunting season is a busy time as Lester processes game. ❄ Since the market doesn't ship, you'll just have to visit Blanco to get some of that good sausage!

612 Chandler Street • (830) 833-1194

Hill Country Lavender

Blanco

In 1999 photographer Robb Kendrick, on assignment in southern France, was taken with the beauty of the rows of bushy purple lavender. After talking to the lavender farmers in the area, he learned that the soil and climate were comparable to those of the Texas Hill Country. He returned home and began to experiment with planting different varieties of lavender on his acreage near Blanco. ❋ With advice from the French farmers, he and his wife, Jeannie Ralston, planted two acres of lavender in 1999. The crop grew fabulously, and the next year they planted more plants. By the spring of 2002, a total of 6,000 plants bloomed during the blooming season from mid-May into early July. In 2004 Rob and Jeannie installed a commercial-size distilling facility to create lavender oil from buds and stems. They also began to host local seminars on growing lavender, paving the way for a new Hill Country industry. ❋ Hill Country Lavender was purchased by Tasha Brieger in 2006 when its original owners decided to move to Mexico. Tasha, formerly Robb's photo assistant, had worked on the farm for six years when she was made its manager. ❋ With the change in ownership, the farm was moved to its current location on a two-acre hilltop behind McCall Creek Farms Market just over three miles north of Blanco. From the end of May to the end of June, you can cut your own lavender at the farm. The store, snuggled into the lavender field, offers more than seventy lavender-related products for sale. Hill Country Lavender products are also available year round at Brieger Pottery, owned by Tasha's parents and located on the town square in Blanco.

4524 N. U.S. 281 • (830) 833-2294 • www.hillcountrylavender.com

McCall Creek Farms Market

Blanco

After several years of growing cut flowers for the wholesale trade, Mark and Cathie Itz, both raised in agriculture in the Texas Hill Country, decided to switch to produce. In 2000 they opened the McCall Creek Farms Market, embracing their dream of operating a real country market. Located several miles north of Blanco, the market has a devoted following of folks who drive for miles to purchase

the farm's quality fruits and vegetables as well as produce from surrounding farms, such as Amador Farms lettuces. ❀ McCall Creek Farms Market sells seasonal produce and peaches grown on the farm as well as blackberries grown at Itz Gardens, the farm of Mark's father, Melvin Itz. The kitchen inside the market is where Cathie makes an eagerly awaited daily supply of fresh breads, pies, cookies, four varieties of homemade ice cream, and peach cobbler in season. And her whole-grain and nut granola is truly the best you'll ever eat. The Itzes' youngest son, Skylar, has a flock of free-range chickens and sells his hens' eggs at the market. Patrons can also buy salsas made by other family members, locally produced jams and pickles, pecans, CKC Farms cheeses, and Loncito's Grass-Fed Lamb products. ❀ McCall Creek Farms consists of land that Cathie inherited from her father's ranch, Conn Ranch, which originated in 1874 with a State of Texas land grant. Through the generations, the ranch grew in size and was inducted into the Texas Family Land Heritage Registry in 1998. Mark and Cathie live in the home that her great-grandfather, J. Lee Conn, built on the ranch about 1905. ❀ Mark sums up the life of a farmer succinctly: "We're not billionaires here—just real farmers trying to keep the land in the family."

4524 N. U.S. 281 • (830) 833-0442 • www.mccallcreekfarms.com

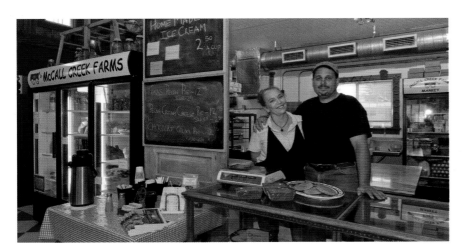

ICEBERG WEDGE WITH BLUE CHEESE DRESSING

Don't discount iceberg lettuce as an inferior salad green. Nothing makes a more impressive salad than a tall quarter wedge of iceberg lettuce draped with a great blue cheese dressing. Fresh-from-the-ground iceberg has a marvelous flavor all its own and the ultimate crispness to be found in a salad green.

Yield: 4 servings

1 head iceberg lettuce, cored, sliced into 4 wedges, and well chilled
6 slices applewood-smoked bacon, cooked until crisp and chopped into fine dice
4 ounces (1 cup) crumbled blue cheese

Blue Cheese Dressing

½ cup real mayonnaise
½ cup sour cream
1 teaspoon celery salt
2 teaspoons freshly squeezed lime juice
2 teaspoons Dijon-style mustard
1 tablespoon minced onion
1 tablespoon minced fresh Mexican mint marigold, or substitute minced fresh tarragon
1 teaspoon Tabasco
3 ounces blue cheese

Make the Blue Cheese Dressing. In work bowl of food processor, combine all ingredients except the blue cheese. Process until smooth and well blended. Add the blue cheese and pulse just until the cheese is blended; leave some small lumps. Refrigerate until ready to serve.

To serve the salad, cut a small slice off the bottom of each wedge so that it will stand flat on the plate. Place one wedge on each serving plate. Drape a portion of the dressing across each wedge, allowing the dressing to pool slightly on the plates, then scatter some of the bacon and crumbled blue cheese over the lettuce and around the plate.

(Terry Thompson-Anderson)

29

BREWHOUSE BROWN ALE AND CHEDDAR CHEESE SOUP WITH GARLIC FLOATERS

Real Ale Brewing Company's Brewhouse Brown Ale is a caramel-brown ale made from four kinds of malts and American hops. It's the perfect taste complement in this hearty, delicious soup.

Yield: 10 to 12 servings

¼ cup canola oil

2 medium onions, chopped

3 carrots, peeled and sliced thin

3 celery stalks, chopped

4 baking potatoes (about 2½ pounds), peeled and cut into ½-inch dice

4 jalapeños, seeds and veins removed, minced

⅓ cup whole-grain mustard

1 bottle (12-ounce) Real Ale Brewing Company Brewhouse Brown Ale, or substitute another European-style dark bock beer

2 quarts chicken stock

3½ cups (14 ounces) shredded sharp Cheddar cheese

Salt to taste

1 cup whipping cream

Garlic Floaters

4 cups ½-inch French bread cubes

¾ pound (3 sticks) unsalted butter, melted (1½ cups)

¼ teaspoon salt

2 heaping teaspoons granulated garlic

Make the Garlic Floaters. Preheat oven to 300 degrees. Place the bread cubes in a medium bowl. In a separate bowl, whisk together the melted butter, salt, and granulated garlic. Pour the mixture evenly over the bread cubes and toss quickly, coating well. Turn the bread cubes out in a single layer onto a baking sheet. Bake in preheated oven until cubes are lightly brown and very crisp. Turn out onto a wire rack and cool completely. To store the Garlic Floaters for up to three days, transfer to a container with a tight-fitting lid.

To make the soup, heat the canola oil in a heavy, 6-quart soup pot over medium heat. Add the onions, carrots, celery, and potatoes. Cook, stirring occasionally, until onions are wilted and transparent, about 8 minutes. Add the jalapeños, mustard, beer, and chicken stock. Stir to blend well, cover, and simmer for 30 minutes, or until potatoes are very soft and have started to break apart. Puree the soup in batches in a blender or food processor until completely smooth. Return to a clean pot over medium heat and stir in the cheese. Cook just until the cheese has melted. Add salt to taste. Do not allow the soup to boil once the cheese has been added. Stir in the whipping cream and cook just to heat the cream through. Serve hot, garnished with Garlic Floaters.

(Terry Thompson-Anderson)

Real Ale Brewing Company

Blanco

The Real Ale Brewing Company makes some serious beer in an artisan environment that fosters unique beers. It's all about passion and commitment to the quality of the product. ❧ The company's president, Brad Farbstein, started brewing beer in 1987 as a hobby while he attended the University of Texas at Austin. He loved the whole process of creating beers with great flavor. After working as a marketing director for a craft brewery in Houston, he was able to buy Real Ale in 1998. At that time, it was a tiny brewing company located in the basement of an antique shop on Blanco's town square and produced 600 barrels of beer. In 2007 Brad built a new, state-of-the-art brewery that could produce 30,000 barrels. ❧ The entire staff is totally involved with the products from beginning to end, following an exacting process supervised by plant manager Todd Ehlers and head brewer Tim Schwarz. ❧ With its 60-barrel stainless steel brewing system, the company makes a fabulous lineup of beers using 100 percent malted grain, domestic and imported hops, and crystal-clear water from the Blanco River. Several beers—Rio Blanco Pale Ale, Full Moon Pale Rye Ale, Brewhouse Brown Ale, and Fireman's #4 Blond Ale—are available year round at most bars, restaurants, and grocers in Austin, Houston, Dallas, Fort Worth, San Antonio, and around the Hill Country. The company also produces some unique seasonal brews: Sisyphus Barleywine Ale, Phoenixx Double Extra Special Bitter, Devil's Backbone, Lost Gold IPA, Roggenbier, and Shade-Grown Coffee Porter. ❧ The brewery is open to the public on Friday afternoons, when tours are available.

231 San Saba Court
(830) 833-2534
www.realalebrewing.com

Redbud Café
Blanco

Redbud Café, located on the town square in a building that once housed the hardware store, has all the trappings of a place that's been around forever, despite its relatively recent opening in September of 2009. Sunlight streams in through the old storefront windows, showcasing tables with colorful tablecloths and a menu board on the wall. When the café opens at 10:30, folks filter in with their laptops or newspapers, staking claim to a table. Coffee and conversation set the tone, and many stay till lunchtime! It's a place where you just feel at home. ❀ Proprietors Jon and Jan Brieger, potters by trade, opened Brieger Pottery in 1992 in one side of the old hardware store, and the shop soon became a destination for those seeking fine, handmade pottery. The once-tiny shop now opens into the café, so diners can browse the entire selection of lovely pieces. ❀ The Briegers had no experience in the food industry, but Jan had baked and sold cookies for years to supplement their income from pottery, which, she says, "hasn't always been the most lucrative business." They knew they wanted to open an eatery where the locals could gather, so they hired the best home cooks and created a menu based on comfort foods and fresh, seasonal produce. There are daily specials in addition to soups, salads, sandwiches, wraps, quiches, gourmet burgers, and the marvelous Casbah Platter, which is piled with quinoa tabouli, hummus, olives, feta cheese, and pita bread. The old-fashioned bakery case is loaded with cookies, pastries, and mile-high cakes with luscious icings. ❀ The Briegers' daughter, Tasha, who owns Hill Country Lavender, provides the lavender for the café's wonderful lavender lemonade, an innovative chicken salad with lavender nuances, and tasty lavender-vanilla cupcakes. When the café gets busy, Tasha helps out. It's a genuine family operation. ❀ The selection of beverages ranges from the locally roasted coffee and specialty coffee drinks to lemonade and sodas, beers from Real Ale Brewing Company (many of them on tap), and wines from local wineries. ❀ The café is open until 9 p.m. on Friday and Saturday evenings, when diners can enjoy dancing and music featuring local musicians.

410 4th Street (on the Square) • (830) 833-0202 • www.redbud-cafe.com

GINGER-MOLASSES COOKIES

Yield: About 4½ dozen large cookies

3 cups butter, softened
4 cups firmly packed light brown sugar
¾ cup molasses
4 eggs, well beaten
9 cups all-purpose flour
2 tablespoons plus 2 teaspoons baking soda
2 teaspoons salt
2 teaspoons ground ginger
2 teaspoons ground cloves
Granulated sugar

Preheat oven to 350 degrees. Lightly grease 3 or 4 large baking sheets and set aside.

Combine the softened butter, brown sugar, molasses, and eggs in bowl of electric mixer. Beginning on low speed and increasing to medium-high speed when ingredients are blended, beat the mixture for about 5 minutes, or until fluffy and light. In a separate bowl mix together the dry ingredients, whisking to blend well. Add the dry ingredients to the egg mixture and beat until well blended.

Roll the dough into balls about the size of a large egg, or 3 ounces each. Flatten each ball and coat with granulated sugar. Place on prepared baking sheets, allowing 1⅓ inches between each cookie. Bake in preheated oven for 14 minutes. Cool on wire racks.

(Redbud Café)

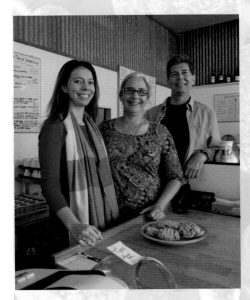

CHILI CORN CREPES

Chef Weber serves these crepes on a bed of pureed black beans surrounded by grilled squash.

Yield: 4 servings (8 to 10 crepes)

1 cup yellow cornmeal
¼ cup all-purpose flour
1 tablespoon ancho chili powder
1 teaspoon salt
1 large egg
¾ cup whole milk
1 tablespoon melted butter

Chipotle Sauce

2 chipotle chilies in adobo, chopped
1 cup whipping cream
1 teaspoon salt

Lime-Butter Sauce

¾ cup freshly squeezed lime juice
6 ounces (1½ sticks) unsalted butter, cut into ½-inch dice

Filling

2 (6-ounce) spiny lobster tails
1 cup lump crabmeat
Butter for sautéing
1 large avocado, peeled and cut into ½-inch dice
1 large ripe mango, peeled and cut into ½-inch dice
1 teaspoon salt
1 teaspoon black pepper

Combine the cornmeal, flour, chili powder, and salt in a small mixing bowl. In a separate bowl, combine the egg, milk, and butter. Add to the cornmeal mixture, blending well. Let batter stand for 30 minutes.

Heat a nonstick 6-inch omelet or sauté pan over medium heat until a drop of water placed in the pan dances and evaporates almost immediately. Ladle 2 tablespoons of the crepe batter into the center of the hot pan and swirl the pan quickly until the batter covers the bottom of the pan. Cook 30 seconds, gently flip the crepe, and cook an additional 30 seconds on the other side. Repeat until all batter is used.

(continued)

Uptown Blanco Arts & Entertainment Restaurant

Blanco

It's not every day that someone comes along and buys an entire block of a Hill Country town. But that's exactly what happened in Blanco when Renee Benson bought the 300 block of Main Street on the town square. ❀ Renee, daughter of New Orleans Saints owner Tom Benson and a thirty-year resident of the Hill Country, got the idea for an arts and entertainment complex in 1999, when she noticed a group of buildings in various states of disrepair. She began buying and renovating the properties as they became available. ❀ The restaurant, housed in a former general merchandise store, opened in 2006. The renovation was extensive, creating a marvelous space reminiscent of a grand restaurant of the late nineteenth century, when the building was erected. With breakfast, lunch, and dinner menus, the restaurant enhances the experience of patrons attending other Uptown Blanco venues, such as the theater (located in the adjacent building), textile studio, tavern, ballroom, art center, frame shop, and courtyard. ❀ The Uptown Blanco kitchen is under the direction of Chef Robert Webber, who

has worked with some of the state's premier chefs, including Tim Keating and Bruce Auden. Chef Webber's menus are a delight—an eclectic romp through the various cuisines that have influenced his style, such as Cajun, Southwestern, and East Asian. Many of his dishes feature products from local farms.

317 Main Street •
(830) 833-0738 •
www.uptownblanco.com

Make the Chipotle Sauce. Combine all ingredients in a small saucepan and cook over medium heat until cream is thickened enough to coat the back of a spoon. Strain through a fine strainer and set aside; keep warm.

Make the Lime-Butter Sauce. In a small saucepan over medium-high heat, reduce the lime juice to about 2 tablespoons. Reduce heat to low and whisk in the butter, one piece at a time, until all has been added (the sauce will be thin). Remove from heat and set aside; keep warm, but not hot, or the sauce will separate.

To make the filling, split the lobster tails in half and remove the meat; dice and set aside. Pick through the crabmeat to remove any shell fragments; set aside.

To assemble the crepes, place crepes on a baking sheet in a warm oven. Sauté the lobster meat in a small amount of butter. Add the crabmeat, mango, and avocado; season with salt and pepper. Cook just until warm. Remove from heat and stir in the Lime-Butter Sauce. Divide the lobster mixture into 8 equal portions and place in the center of the crepes; roll crepes up and place on serving plates. Drizzle Chipotle Cream over the crepes and serve warm.

(Uptown Blanco Arts & Entertainment Restaurant)

MUSHROOMS AND AURELIA'S CHORIZO IN TRIPLE SHERRY CREAM SAUCE

This recipe makes a pretty sensational party dish.

Yield: 4 to 6 servings as a finger food

3 tablespoons pure olive oil
2 large shallots
3 large garlic cloves, minced
5 ounces small white button mushrooms, halved
3 ounces shiitake mushrooms, sliced
¼ teaspoon crushed red pepper flakes
2 cups medium-dry sherry (amontillado), divided
3 thyme sprigs
1 link Aurelia's Chorizo (about 2½ ounces), sliced very thin
2 cups whipping cream
1 Knorr chicken bouillon cube
Salt and freshly ground black pepper to taste
½ cup cream sherry
French baguette slices, slightly toasted

Heat olive oil in a heavy 10-inch skillet over medium heat. When oil is hot, add the shallots and garlic; sauté until shallots are wilted and transparent, about 5 minutes. Do not allow garlic to brown. Stir in the mushrooms and crushed red pepper. Cook, stirring often, until mushroom liquid has evaporated and mushrooms are limp, about 6 to 7 minutes. Add ⅔ cup of the dry sherry and the thyme. Stir in the chorizo. Cook over medium-high heat, stirring often, until sherry is reduced to a mere glaze, about 5 minutes. Repeat two more times, using ⅔ cup of sherry and reducing to a glaze each time. Stir in the whipping cream, scraping up any browned bits from the bottom and sides of the pan. Add the bouillon cube and stir to dissolve. Season to taste with salt and freshly ground black pepper. Cook over medium heat, stirring often, until cream is thickened, about 6 minutes. Add the cream sherry and stir to blend well. Adjust seasoning. Remove from heat and discard the thyme sprigs. Transfer to a shallow serving dish and serve hot with toasted baguette slices.

(Terry Thompson-Anderson)

Aurelia's Chorizo

Boerne

Aurelia's Chorizo was born from Leslie Horne's addiction to authentic Spanish chorizo, which a friend smuggled from Spain twenty years ago. It was a classic case of love at first bite— a bite that started Leslie, a former homemaker, on an odyssey into the world of making this dry-cured sausage. ❄ Leslie researched recipes and began to make the chorizo for friends. But it was hard to cold-smoke the sausage properly at home. So a determined Leslie went to Spain in 2000, touring chorizo plants and learning how to make the sausage commercially. When she finally found a processor with a kindred adventurous spirit, they worked together to build the smoking and drying facility according to USDA specs. ❄ With the formula finally perfected, Leslie began producing Aurelia's Chorizo in 2006. The sausage is made to very high standards. Full cuts of pork and beef chuck are used with absolutely no fillers or trimmings. Garlic is freshly ground for each batch of the sausage, and Leslie imports pimentón—the smoked paprika that is so important to the sausage's deep, rich flavor—from the La Vera region of Spain, known for its fine paprika. The smoking, aging, and drying process takes an entire month, and the result is a really fabulous, very authentic Spanish chorizo. Aurelia's Chorizo is available at Central Market stores and at Spec's Liquor Stores in Austin.

(830) 446-1325 • www.aureliaschorizo.com

Bear Moon Bakery

Boerne

The stated mission of Paula Hayward's community bakery is "to nourish the Community Heart." Mission accomplished, Paula. ❄ Step inside the bakery in the wee hours of the morning and your senses are immediately aroused by the aromas of wonderful things baking in the massive ovens in back. By 7 a.m. the pastry cases are loaded with pastries, cookies, cakes, scones, muffins, teacakes, pies of every description, and such rare finds as Kugelhopf, a light yeast cake of Austrian derivation filled with raisins, candied fruits, and nuts and generously dusted with powdered sugar. ❄ The place is bustling with sleepy-eyed folks picking up preordered trays of pastries, cookies, or cakes. Others are seated at tables overlooking Boerne's busy Main Street, enjoying their coffee (consistently voted as "the best coffee in Boerne") and breakfast pastries or items from the breakfast buffet. A favorite is the Jalapeño Hog, a smoked sausage in pastry with cheese and sliced jalapeños—the bakery sells over 10,000 per week! ❄ By mid-morning, when the focus shifts to lunch preparation, Bear Moon once again fills up with folks hungry for the from-scratch soups, an array of salads, and sandwiches served on homemade breads. ❄ Housed in a building dating from the early 1900s, the bakery opened in the 1960s under the name Hill Country Bakery. In the 1980s Boerne's longtime mayor, Patrick Heath, was the baker. Paula—a photographer, artist, and chef who found food

to be the niche she was seeking—purchased and renamed the bakery in 1995. ❄ A strong believer in community involvement and sustainability, Paula cuts energy consumption with a mix of light-

Cheezy Pigs
1.65

ing and timers and recycles plastics, metal, glass, and newsprint. All produce trimmings and coffee grounds are composted. The bakery grows its own herbs and flowers, uses roof run-off water for irrigation, and works with local farmers and growers. ❄ Bear Moon, a favorite among locals, has been named "Best Bakery" for over eleven years. It is a must-visit stop in Boerne and has been featured in *Texas Monthly* and *Texas Highways*, boosting its already excellent reputation.

401 S. Main Street • (830) 816-2327

APPLE CAKE

This delicious confection is a special Christmas item at the bakery, but it's easy to prepare at home all year round.

Yield: One 9-inch cake

3 cups all-purpose flour
1 teaspoon baking soda
½ teaspoon salt
2 cups sugar
1 cup vegetable oil
3 large eggs
1 teaspoon vanilla
1 cup chopped pecans
4 medium Granny Smith apples, peeled, cored, and chopped (3 cups)

Glaze

1 cup brown sugar
⅓ cup butter
⅓ cup milk

Preheat the oven to 350 degrees. Butter and flour a 9-inch springform cake pan; set aside. Sift together the flour, baking soda, and salt. In bowl of electric mixer at medium speed, beat together the sugar, vegetable oil, eggs, and vanilla until pale yellow and smooth. Beat in the flour mixture, a third at a time, scraping down the sides of the bowl after each addition. Mix in the pecans and apples. The batter will be very thick. Turn out into the prepared springform pan and bake in preheated oven for 45 to 55 minutes, or until a toothpick inserted in the middle of the cake comes out clean. Cool in pan for 10 minutes, remove sides and bottom of pan, and place cake on cooling rack. Cool completely before glazing.

While the cake is baking, prepare the glaze. In a 2-quart saucepan, bring all ingredients to a boil, reduce heat, and simmer for 5 minutes. Brush or spoon over the cooled cake.

(Bear Moon Bakery)

PANCETTA-WRAPPED PORK TENDERLOIN WITH BASIL-POTATO CRESPELLE STUFFED WITH PORTABELLA MUSHROOMS AND TOMATO–OLIVE OIL SAUCE

Yield: 4 servings

2 trimmed pork tenderloins (about 1½ pounds total), silver skin removed

Salt and freshly ground black pepper

¼ cup thinly sliced basil leaves

1 cup chopped fresh mozzarella

16 thin slices of pancetta or bacon, rolled thin with a rolling pin

Olive oil

Potato Crespelle

2 large baking potatoes, baked until fork tender, cooled, and peeled

3 eggs

1¼ cups milk

2 tablespoons canola oil

Pinch of freshly grated nutmeg

Pinch of ground ginger

½ cup all-purpose flour

1 tablespoon minced basil leaves

Salt and ground white pepper

Olive oil

Portabella Filling

2 large portabella mushrooms, stems removed

2 tablespoons balsamic vinegar

½ cup olive oil

Salt and black pepper to taste

12 pieces pencil asparagus, trimmed and blanched in salt water until crisp-tender

Shredded Parmesan cheese

Tomato–Olive Oil Sauce

4 Roma tomatoes, chopped

1 red bell pepper, chopped

1 tablespoon peeled and crushed garlic

½ teaspoon crushed red pepper flakes

½ cup chopped red onion

1 cup olive oil

¼ cup red wine vinegar

1 rosemary sprig

Salt and freshly ground black pepper to taste

(continued)

Cypress Grille

Boerne

Cypress Grille is entered through the historic Napa Building amid the hustle and bustle of Boerne's busy Main Street. Opened in 2006, the restaurant was the brainchild of Paul Thompson, business partner Tom Stevens, and Tom's wife, Shanda. The trio wanted to serve great food with fabulous wines, all in a comfortable environment. ❀ Cypress Grille definitely has one of the Hill Country's most sophisticated wine lists and a wine room that is not to be missed. And that fabulous real draft root beer is just the ticket to quench a big thirst after shopping Boerne's Main Street. ❀ The restaurant has been a success since its opening, with a menu featuring an eclectic mix of "upscale down-home" offerings and downright upscale treasures. The lunch menu features appetizers that present an array of innovative flavors, a large selection of salads and sandwiches, soups, a daily lunch special, and, of course, housemade desserts. The dinner menu pulls out all the stops, from a lengthy selection of appetizers

(including—be still my heart—foie gras with a port reduction!) to steaks and chops, seafood, poultry dishes, and even more desserts. Cypress Grille has become one of Boerne's most popular dining destinations. ❀ Paul spent many years in California, where he learned the craft of butchering and also gained an extensive knowledge of wines. After returning to Texas, he graduated from the Texas Culinary Academy in Austin. Tom, the executive chef at Cypress Grille, graduated from the Culinary Institute of America in Hyde Park, New York. Shanda runs the "front of the house," greeting customers with a smile that says, "Welcome to our table."

170 S. Main Street, Suite 200 • (830) 248-1353
• www.cypressgrilleboerne.com

Make the Tomato–Olive Oil Sauce. Place all ingredients in a heavy 3-quart saucepan over medium-low heat. Slowly simmer for 25 minutes. Remove the rosemary sprig and allow sauce to cool slightly, then pour into blender and puree until smooth. Adjust seasoning as needed. Strain and return to saucepan over very low heat; keep warm.

Butterfly the pork tenderloins from the tip to the tail, slowly unrolling them. Using a meat pounder, lightly pound both tenderloins into rectangles about ¼ inch thick. Season to taste with salt and black pepper. Scatter the basil strips over the meat, then top each with an equal portion of the mozzarella. Starting at the long side, roll up each tenderloin tightly. Lay the pancetta strips out, slightly overlapping, and set the rolled tenderloins on the pancetta strips. Roll up the strips very tight, covering the tenderloin with the pancetta. Season with salt and black pepper and set aside. Preheat oven to 350 degrees.

Make the Portabella Filling. Place the mushrooms on a char grill and brush with vinegar and olive oil. Season with salt and black pepper. Place the asparagus on the grill and season with olive oil, salt, and black pepper. Remove the asparagus as soon as it has grill marks. When the mushrooms are slightly wilted, cut them into thin strips. Set asparagus and mushroom strips aside.

To make the Potato Crespelles, push the potatoes through a ricer or grate into a large bowl. Add remaining ingredients except olive oil and stir batter to blend well. Allow to rest for 30 minutes.

While batter is resting, heat a very thin glaze of olive oil in a heavy 12-inch skillet over medium-high heat. When oil is very hot, sear the tenderloins on all sides until browned. Transfer to a baking dish and finish cooking in preheated oven for about 20 minutes.

While tenderloins are roasting, cook the Potato Crespelles. Heat a 10-inch nonstick pan and oil lightly with the olive oil. Pour in ⅓ cup of the batter and swirl pan to distribute batter evenly. Lightly brown, flip, and cook an additional 20 seconds; remove from pan. Set aside and keep warm; repeat with the remaining batter.

When the tenderloins are cooked, remove from oven and set aside to rest while assembling the Potato Crespelles.

Lay crespelles on work surface and divide the asparagus and mushroom strips among them. Scatter a generous portion of Parmesan cheese over the vegetables, then roll the crespelles up tight. Place 2 crespelles on each serving plate. Slice the tenderloins about ½ inch thick and fan out 3 to 4 slices, slightly overlapping the crespelles on each plate. Top with Tomato–Olive Oil Sauce and serve at once.

(Cypress Grille)

CHOCOLATE CHESS PIE

Yield: One 9-inch pie

Unbaked pastry dough for 9-inch pie
1 cup melted butter or margarine
⅓ cup cocoa
1 tablespoon vanilla
2 cups sugar
3 eggs

Preheat oven to 325 degrees. Fit the pastry into a 9-inch pie pan. Flute the edges as desired, or use the tines of a fork to press the edges onto the rim of the pan. Keep pastry refrigerated until ready to bake.

Combine butter, cocoa, vanilla, and sugar in bowl of stand mixer. Beat until smooth and well blended, about 3 minutes. Add the eggs, one at a time, beating after each addition until blended. Beat for an additional 3 minutes, or until mixture is smooth and creamy. Pour into pastry shell and bake in preheated oven for 50 to 60 minutes, or until set. The filling will puff up during baking, but will deflate as it cools. Cool on wire rack, then chill in refrigerator before slicing.

(Patio Café)

Patio Café

Brady

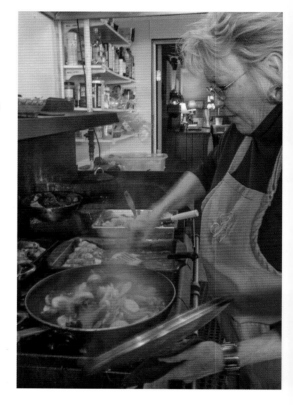

Situated on Brady's town square, the Patio Café is a cozy spot to grab a great home-cooked lunch. Owner Barbara Bolton and her life partner, James Minor, restored the old 1930s-era Greyhound bus station and opened a gift shop. Folks liked to gather in one corner where Barbara had placed three tables and a coffee maker, so she added more tables and began serving a few sandwiches. ❧ It wasn't long before she dropped the gifts entirely and became a full-fledged luncheon spot. "I've been blessed with a great group of local customers," she says, "and I have many travelers who try to make it to Brady for lunch." Some of her regular customers like to be called when their favorite dishes are on the menu, and many request certain dishes when they are bringing guests. ❧ The menu features three specials that change daily—a soup, a quiche, and a blue-plate-special. Popular sandwiches include a Reuben, French Dip, Philly Cheese Steak, and a Mexican sandwich that is Barbara's own creation, made with avocado, pico de gallo, turkey, and ham or bacon. There's also a low-carb salad and homemade chicken salad. ❧ But be sure to save room for Barbara's legendary made-from-scratch desserts, such as apple enchiladas, buttermilk pie (with additions like coconut or almonds), chocolate chess pie, and bread pudding with cinnamon sauce. She loves to collect new recipes, but the best in her collection are those from her mother and grandmother, a wonderful country cook.

212 N. Church Street • (325) 597-0569

Fain's Honey

Buchanan Dam

Fain's Honey is a small, unassuming place eleven miles east of Llano. Here you can purchase all of the company's products, but you'll also find them in supermarkets throughout the state. ❦ The company was established in 1926 by H. E. Fain, who kept several hives and began selling honey from unlabeled fruit jars. He was meticulous

about the cleanliness and appearance of his honey and soon gained a reputation as a supplier of top-quality honey from 175 colonies of bees. During the Depression, when sugar was a luxury, he found a ready market for his honey. ❦ In 2005 Keith Fain, a grandson of the company's founder, acquired Fain's Honey, becoming the third generation of Fains to produce honey. Keith and his

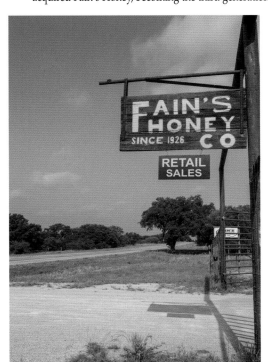

wife, Debra, expanded the product line to include raw native honey, honey butter spreads (such as a delicious jalapeño variety), ribbon cane syrup, and sorghum molasses, all of which are available through the Web site. ❦ Today Keith has about 1,000 bee colonies, but the products are produced in a small-scale, hands-on operation. He doesn't feed his bees any substances to lengthen the production season. The company's motto is "Fain's honey doesn't pretend to be a gourmet honey, rather just a wholesome, natural Texas honey product." There are two key words there that sum up why it's so good—natural and Texas!

14817 E. State Hwy. 29 • (512) 793-2491 • www.fainshoney.com

ARUGULA AND BIBB LETTUCE SALAD WITH FIGS, GOAT CHEESE, AND HONEY-LEMON VINAIGRETTE

The vinaigrette for this salad can be made a day ahead and refrigerated.

Yield: 4 servings

Equal portions arugula and Bibb lettuce for 4 portions, torn into bite-size pieces
12 fresh figs, halved (or quartered if figs are large)
1 cup crumbled semi-hard goat cheese
Pecan pieces

Honey-Lemon Vinaigrette

1 teaspoon minced lemon zest
¼ cup freshly squeezed lemon juice
¼ teaspoon kosher salt or fine-grain sea salt
2 tablespoons Fain's Honey
3 tablespoon chopped fresh chives
½ cup extra-virgin olive oil
Freshly ground black pepper to taste

Make the Honey-Lemon Vinaigrette. Combine all ingredients except the olive oil and pepper in work bowl of food processor fitted with steel blade. Process until well blended. With processor running, add the olive oil in a slow, steady stream through the feed tube. Add the black pepper and process for about 15 additional seconds. Transfer to a storage container and refrigerate until ready to serve.

To assemble the salad, toss the arugula and Bibb lettuce together. Place equal portions of the mixed greens on individual salad plates. Arrange some of the figs on each salad. Drizzle a portion of the Honey-Lemon Vinaigrette over the salads, scatter ¼ cup of the crumbled goat cheese over each, and garnish with a few pecan pieces.

(Terry Thompson-Anderson)

Hairston Creek Farm
Burnet

Gary Rowland was no stranger to growing things when he and his wife, Sarah, purchased their thirty-six-acre farm in 1990. Gary had grown up in the melon fields of East Texas and worked at one of the Texas A&M Agricultural Experiment Stations researching vegetables. ❈ Hairston Creek Farm is a small sustainable family farm that specializes in organic vegetables, herbs, and fruit. Certified organic by the Texas Department of Agriculture since 1993, the farm consists of seventeen acres of mixed vegetables covering the gamut from asparagus to zucchini as well as strawberries and blackberries. A small apiary improves crop pollination, and the two Rowland children tend the bees and bottle the honey. Using excess fresh fruit and produce, the family makes jams, jellies, and pesto in their state-certified commercial kitchen, and they raise cage-free chickens and market "yard" eggs. ❈ Before Sarah lost a long battle with breast cancer in 2012, she was deeply concerned about people's general attitude toward food. "They tend to think of food as they do water and electricity—it's just there," she said. "They have no idea where it comes from!" Gary remains totally dedicated to practicing sustainable agriculture and growing organic: "It just makes sense to grow organically—on a family level, community level, national level, and global level. With every acre of organically grown vegetables and livestock, that's an acre free of chemical fertilizers, insecticides, and herbicides. We just need more of those organic acres to clean up the world!"

❈ Saturday mornings are busy times, with the family selling Hairston Creek Farm products at two separate farmer's markets: the Farmer's Market on the Square in Burnet and also the Sunset Valley Farmer's Market in Austin.

4300 CR 335 • (512) 756-8380 • www.hairston-creekfarm.com

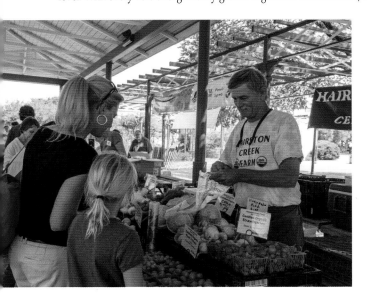

PAN-SEARED GREENS WITH BACON AND BALSAMIC REDUCTION

Pan-seared fresh greens make a heavenly winter side dish, especially when made with Hairston Creek Farm's perky, leafy greens. For the best flavor, do use the bacon drippings!

Yield: 4 servings

3 tablespoons bacon drippings

3 large garlic cloves, cut into thin slices

10 cups mixed red chard and green kale, torn into bite-size pieces, with thick mid-ribs removed and discarded

Balsamic Reduction (see recipe below)

6 slices peppered bacon, cooked until crisp, drained well, and chopped into fine dice

Balsamic Reduction

2 cups balsamic vinegar

1 cup firmly packed light brown sugar

Make the Balsamic Reduction. Stir together the balsamic vinegar and brown sugar in a heavy 2-quart saucepan over medium heat. Bring to a boil; reduce heat to a simmer and cook until the liquid is thick and syrupy, about 30 minutes. Cool and transfer to a plastic squeeze bottle. (You won't need all of the reduction for the batch of greens. The remaining reduction may be refrigerated for up to three weeks.)

Heat the bacon drippings in a heavy, deep-sided 12-inch skillet over medium heat. When the fat is hot, add the sliced garlic and greens, tossing to coat with the drippings. Cook, tossing constantly, until the greens begin to wilt. Squeeze some of the Balsamic Reduction onto the greens and continue to cook, tossing, until the greens are wilted but still crisp. Add the chopped bacon and toss to distribute. Serve hot.

(Terry Thompson-Anderson)

Tea-Licious

Burnet

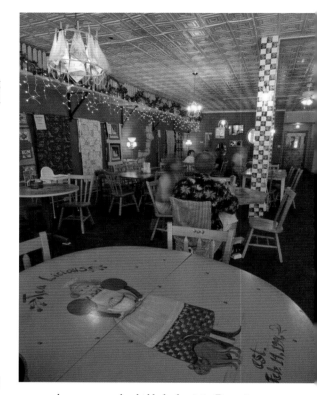

Owner Vicki McLeod opened her first tearoom in Burnet on Valentine's Day of 1996. She and her husband, Sam, had moved to their ranch outside of Burnet after a long tenure in Montgomery, where Vicki had taught high-school English. After eighteen months of cabin fever on the ranch and no luck in finding a teaching position, Vicki had the idea of opening a tearoom. Sam wasn't terribly excited about the venture but went along with it, asking her only that she not lose too much money. After all, he thought, there are only a few thousand residents in the whole town. Little did he know what the future and Vicki's famous Chicken Salad would bring! ❀ That first day the tearoom drew more than a hundred customers, and word spread quickly about the delicious array of sandwiches, specialty salads, quiches, soups, and an awesome loaded baked potato. Desserts range from homemade pies to cheesecakes and individual Chocolate Volcano cakes. ❀ Within two years Vicki had moved into a 5,000-square-foot historic building on the square. With the expansion came a new gift shop–boutique known as Giftique, where Vicki sells many one-of-a-kind, must-have items as well as her Tea-Licious Gourmet Sweet Pickles. Sam eventually retired from his career in medical equipment manufacturing to help run the tearoom! ❀ Billed as "the little tearoom on Burnet's historic square," Tea-Licious is a charming respite from browsing in the community's unique shops. It's a favorite lunch spot of passengers traveling on the *Hill Country Flyer,* an authentic steam locomotive–powered excursion train that the Austin Steam Train Association runs between Cedar Park and Burnet on weekends from January through May and on select weekends in December when Burnet is fully decked out in Christmas finery. There's ample time for shopping and a visit to Tea-Licious before the "All Aboard" signals the return trip with shopping bags full of goodies in tow and memories of a great meal.

216 S. Main Street • (512) 756-7636 • www.tea-licious.com

Camp Verde General Store & Restaurant

Camp Verde

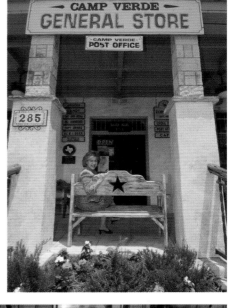

The Camp Verde General Store has a long and colorful history, very much intertwined with the settlement of the Texas frontier. It was established in 1857 by an enterprising man named John Williams, who saw the opportunity to supply provisions to the nearby army outpost on the north bank of Verde Creek. The fort is best known as the headquarters of a corps of imported camels, part of an army experiment in using these animals for military purposes. ❀ In 1858 the store was acquired by Charles Schreiner and his brother-in-law, Casper Real, who obtained a contract to sell beef and wool to the fort. As the operation grew, they offered other items for sale, such as sewing kits, foodstuffs from the surrounding farms, paper and writing materials, blankets, saddle equipment, and eventually liquor (which was forbidden on the fort grounds). A post office operated on the premises in 1858. The store became a gathering place for the local settlers. ❀ Closed during the Civil War, the store reopened in 1887, and a small community began to grow up around it. Numerous owners operated the store after the original structure was destroyed by floodwaters in the early 1900s. ❀ By 2003 the building was in need of repair and restoration when Cynthia Grossman and her husband purchased a ranch above the old site of Camp Verde. Jokingly, their real estate agent asked if they'd like to buy the old store. But Cynthia was intrigued by its history and possibilities and did, indeed, buy it. ❀ Camp Verde General Store has been lovingly restored, and today it operates as a retail store and restaurant. Attractive upscale boutique items, kitchenware, candles, home accessories, jewelry, soaps, food products, artwork, luggage, and oodles of other must-have items are sold in the two-story retail space.

❀ The restaurant offers an eclectic menu of salads, sandwiches, burgers, pizzas, and desserts, plus country favorites. The outdoor patio areas offer the perfect venue for a nice breath of fresh air. Cynthia refers to the Camp Verde General Store as an evolving entity and makes subtle changes often to enhance the experience of visiting there.

285 Camp Verde Road East •
(830) 634-7722 • www.campverdegeneral
store.com

CAMP VERDE

Cherokee Grocery
Cherokee

Cherokee Grocery is one of the most notable places in Cherokee, where many of the buildings are boarded up and in various degrees of decay. You'll always find pitchers of sweet tea on the counter, and favorites like lemon icebox pie and banana pudding are available on top of the old meat case. The grocery opened in 1892 as a much-needed feed and dry goods store in the rural area. ❄ Cherokee native Sue Rhoades and her late husband, Herman, bought the store in 1985. But with the opening of supermarkets and discount stores in the area, Cherokee Grocery sold fewer and fewer groceries. So Sue began to make sandwiches, then homemade bread for the sandwiches. ❄ Sue still sells groceries, mainly staples, but now she serves breakfast and lunch.

She arrives at the store every morning at 6:15 to be ready for the customers who start gathering a little before 7:00 for their morning coffee. She makes salads, burgers on homemade buns, and anything else she thinks of that folks might like. In addition to the pimento cheese sandwiches, her chicken salad is legendary, and she won't part with the recipe either! And we can't forget those homemade pies, cookies, puddings, peanut brittle, and divine milkshakes. ❄ Cherokee Grocery is a place where all the locals and transplants gather to catch up on the latest gossip. Also among her regulars are vendors of every sort who travel Highway 16. ❄ The store hasn't changed much over the years. It still has the original counters with glass-fronted bins that once held flour, meal, and beans. A modern scale was added in 1911 that Sue still uses. Taped to the side of the old scale are signed chits for items needed before payday. Customers still maintain charge accounts with the store, and their account cards are stored in an ancient wooden records box on the counter. ❄ After the store closes at 5:30 p.m., Sue delivers groceries to elderly residents who can't make it to the store. She's also the person the locals call when anything goes wrong. Snake in the house? She'll find someone to dispatch it! ❄ The floors have uneven, squeaky boards, the lights are dim, many of the canned goods are dusty, and the tables are well etched, but Cherokee Grocery and Sue Rhoades are living, working elements of Hill Country history. Stop in and enjoy the great food along with some fabulous stories.

101 N. Indian Street (State Hwy. 16) • (325) 622-4599

CHEROKEE

814, A Texas Bistro

Comfort

814, A Texas Bistro is a great little oasis of dining in the picturesque, sleepy little town of Comfort, where many structures are listed in the National Register of Historic Places and antique shopping is at its best. Owner Millard Kuykendall grew up on a Texas ranch and first experienced the restaurant business as a waiter in his younger years. As he worked his way up through the ranks, he discovered that he had a deep love of food and an affinity for cooking. After a job as a pastry cook, he concentrated on

learning the basics and was eventually hired at Disney World in Orlando, Florida. ❄ When Millard and his family decided to return to the state and open their own restaurant, the historic post office building at 713 High Street was a perfect find. After a bit of remodeling and the addition of an outdoor dining area in the rear, 814 opened for business in 2006. ❄ The menu offers a selection of appetizers, salads, and entrées that changes weekly. Millard builds the menu around the freshest ingredients available, creating simple, honest tastes where fresh food is the star on the plate. "You're coming to my house when you come to 814 Bistro" is the way he sums up the dining experience here. Most of the diners are regulars, and on any given evening you'll find Millard popping out of the kitchen intermittently to chat with folks.

713 High Street • (830) 995-4990 • www.814atexas-bistro.com

JUMBO LUMP CRAB CAKES WITH CHIVE AIOLI

Yield: 8 crab cakes

1 large egg
1 teaspoon Worcestershire sauce
Juice from 1 large lemon
1 cup real mayonnaise
1 teaspoon Creole mustard
1 tablespoon minced flat-leaf parsley
1 pound jumbo lump crabmeat
Finely ground bread crumbs
Salt and black pepper to taste
Melted butter for sautéing

Chive Aioli

¼ cup chopped fresh chives
2 garlic cloves, peeled
½ cup water, or more as needed
1 cup real mayonnaise
Salt and black pepper to taste

Whisk the egg in a large mixing bowl until frothy. Add the Worcestershire sauce, lemon juice, mayonnaise, mustard, and parsley; whisk to blend well. Gently fold in the crabmeat, taking care not to break up the lumps. Add the bread crumbs a little at a time, just enough to bind the mixture together. Add salt and pepper to taste. Divide the crab mixture into 8 equal portions and pat into cakes.

Make the Chive Aioli. Combine the chives, garlic, and water in work bowl of food processor fitted with steel blade; process until smooth. Strain the puree through a fine strainer into a mixing bowl. Stir in the mayonnaise and whisk until smooth, adding additional water if the mixture is too thick. Season to taste with salt and pepper; set aside.

Sauté the crab cakes in melted butter over medium heat for 2 minutes per side, or until golden brown. Serve with the Chive Aioli.

(814, A Texas Bistro)

HIGH'S CHICKEN SALAD

The chicken salad at High's can become addicting, both as a salad and a sandwich filling on one of their yummy bread selections.

Yield: 4 sandwiches or salad servings

6 boneless, skinless chicken breasts, boiled, chilled, and cut into bite-size chunks
1 cup finely diced celery
½ cup thinly sliced green onions
1 cup red seedless grapes
¾ cup good-quality mayonnaise
¾ cup sour cream
Salt and freshly cracked black pepper to taste

Combine all ingredients in a large bowl and stir to blend well. Chill before serving.

(High's Café and Store)

HIGH'S HUMMUS

4 cups canned chick-peas, rinsed and drained
1 tablespoon minced garlic
½ teaspoon red (cayenne) pepper
½ teaspoon ground cumin
½ teaspoon paprika
1 teaspoon kosher salt
2 tablespoons minced flat-leaf parsley
¼ cup fresh lemon juice
2 tablespoons tahini paste
Olive oil
Toasted pita wedges
Greek olives, chopped tomatoes, olive oil, and minced parsley as garnishes

Combine all ingredients except olive oil in work bowl of food processor fitted with steel blade. Add just enough olive oil through the feed tube to get the mixture turning in the bowl (this is important for achieving a very smooth blend). Scrape down the sides of the bowl. As the mixture becomes smooth, slowly add more olive oil to achieve a silky smooth consistency. Process for about 2 to 3 minutes, almost "whipping" the hummus. Serve with toasted pita toasts, Greek olives, and chopped tomatoes. Drizzle olive oil on top and garnish with minced parsley.

(High's Café and Store)

High's Café and Store

Comfort

On Comfort's main shopping arcade, High Street, you'll find High's Café and Store, which offers fabulous coffee (also available in bulk) and coffee drinks. In the cozy interior or out on the front deck, you can enjoy irresistible breakfast pastries or lunchtime specialties such as made-from-scratch soups, salads with house dressings, sandwiches on artisan breads, and tantalizing desserts. Wines are served by the glass in addition to a selection of beers. ❧ High's also sells a great assortment of merchandise—kitchen items, toys and games, greeting cards, books on Texas subjects, pottery, Hill Country olive oil, and pickles and preserves. The impressive wine shop features wines from around the world and from local wineries. Wines produced by Cathie Winmill's Comfort Cellars Winery are sold only here and at the winery. ❧ Owners Brent Ault

and Denise Rabalais started this special place with three sandwiches and some baked goods, along with their gourmet coffees. Brent's association with the food business goes back to his teen years when he and his sister opened an ambitiously large but successful deli in Fort Worth. He eventually moved to Fredericksburg and worked as a baker at some of the city's top restaurants. Denise, a native Houstonian, has a background in architecture and interior design and a passion for good food instilled by her Cajun-French father and Czech mother. After migrating to Fredericksburg, Denise managed the wine list for a large restaurant and met Brent. It's a partnership that works well. ❧ The pair settled on Comfort to start their business because they loved its quirkiness and

genuine small-town feel. Brent does the cooking in the tiny kitchen, and Denise tends the shop, always calling the regulars by name. High's was quickly embraced by the locals, who needed a place to get a good cup of coffee in the morning and a tasty lunch. Now the shopkeepers refer out-of-town customers, and the standing-room-only crowds tell it all.

726 High Street • (830) 995-4995 • www. highscafeandstore.com

SAMMY WALDORF SANDWICH

Yield: 1 sandwich

2 slices Texas toast
⅓ cup grated Fontina cheese
2 strips bacon, fried until crisp

Red Onion Jam

½ cup olive oil
6 red onions, sliced thin
1 cup sugar
2 cups red wine vinegar
1 teaspoon whole mustard seeds
Zest of 1 orange
1 tablespoon salt
2 teaspoons black pepper
6 bay leaves
1 tablespoon dried leaf thyme

Begin by making the Red Onion Jam. Heat olive oil in a large sauté pan. Add onions and sauté until soft. Add remaining ingredients and simmer until mixture is thick and syrupy. Remove from heat and cool. (The jam keeps for several weeks if refrigerated.)

   Butter one side of each Texas toast. Place a slice, buttered side down, in a heated skillet. Pile on the cheese, bacon, and some of the Red Onion Jam. Top with the remaining bread slice, buttered side up. Cook until bread is golden on the bottom, then turn and brown the other side. Slice in half diagonally and serve with a portion of Sammy Waldorf Salad.

SAMMY WALDORF SALAD

Yield: 4 servings

Dressing

3 cups mayonnaise
⅓ cup whole-grain mustard
¼ cup plus 2 tablespoons apple cider vinegar
½ teaspoon celery seed
1 teaspoon salt and 1 teaspoon black pepper
1 tablespoon honey

Salad

2 cups arugula
⅓ cup diced celery
2 tablespoons golden raisins
1 Pink Lady apple, cut into matchstick pieces
⅓ cup toasted walnuts

Whisk together all dressing ingredients until smooth. Combine salad ingredients and toss lightly with the dressing and freshly cracked black pepper. Refrigerate until ready to serve.

(The Plaid Goat)

The Plaid Goat

Comfort

Long a favorite stop for Hill Country antique hounds because of its many unique shops offering quality vintage merchandise, Comfort is becoming a haven for food and wine lovers as well. Brent Ault and Denise Rabalais, owners of High's Café and Store, a popular breakfast and lunch eatery with a wine and foodie shop, felt themselves wanting a nighttime personality—and the town was definitely ready for the concept. ❋ The pair's Plaid Goat added a really hip dimension to High Street with its soaring tin roof and chic, rustic-contemporary design. Enjoy your Hill Country respite either inside or on the delightful covered front patio, complete with the soothing sound of a gently rippling fountain. It's a perfect spot for whiling away those balmy Hill Country evenings. The interior is arranged with an assortment of tables with comfortable chairs, cushy sofas, and overstuffed chairs. A central fireplace offers the warmth of an inviting fire during the winter months. The furnishings and accessories were locally sourced, and the overall ambiance of the space is quite relaxing. "Comfortable elegance" is how Denise described the space she wanted to create. And she was certainly right on the mark. ❋ Patrons can enjoy wines by the glass or bottle and Real Ale Brewing Company beers on tap as well as a nice selection of bottled beers, both domestic and imported. The excellent wine list ranges from sparkling wines to dessert wines with selections from Texas and around the globe. Brent and Denise wanted to avoid labeling the Plaid Goat as a wine bar or a bistro. It's just a great place where people can enjoy camaraderie with friends around libations and select from a great little menu of appetizers, salads, and desserts, plus divine nightly specials that Brent conjures up. It's difficult to decide on just two or three of the menu offerings, all of which are shining examples of his culinary talents, so bring a crowd and order one of each. Sharing is encouraged! Open Thursday through Saturday and on Sunday (see Web site for hours).

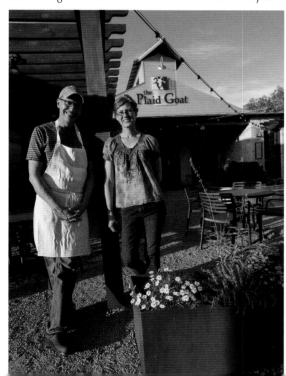

708 High Street • (830) 995-2015 • www.theplaidgoatcomfort.com

Duchman Family Winery

Driftwood

Passion is the driving force behind most things Italian, and the Duchman Family Winery is no exception. When Stan and Lisa Duchman traveled around Italy to explore the many grape varietals used in the production of Italian wines, they were smitten by the powerful flavors and lusty acidity of Old World wines made from varietals like sangiovese, dolcetto, aglianico, vermentino, and nero d'Avola. ❀ The Duchmans had met in Houston while Lisa was in optometry school and Stan was in medical school. After they settled into their respective careers, an Italian neighbor told them of his plan to move to the Hill Country and open a winery with an Italian restaurant on the property. He invited the Duchmans to be his business partners, and after much discussion, the couple decided it would be an exciting challenge and signed on. ❀ "We tasted the wines being produced all over Texas and noticed that our favorites were those made from Mediterranean varietals," Stan recalls. "They were also the varietals that seemed to thrive best in the Texas terroir." The partners worked with viticultural consultant Bobby Cox and growers in the Texas High Plains to accomplish their goal of producing Italian-style wines from grapes that not only thrive well in Texas but yield superior fruit. The concept worked, and the winery was the first in Texas to produce many of the classic Italian wines like vermentino, dulcet, and montepulciano. In 2010 the winery's dolcetto won a double gold medal at the prestigious San Francisco International Wine Competition, quite an accomplishment for a young winery. ❀ The Duchmans are now the sole owners of the estate. The original winemaker, the late Mark Penna, designed the winemaking facilities and formulated the wines. Dave Reilly, Duchman's head winemaker, is doing a stellar job of continuing Mark's vision of producing fine wines from Texas-grown fruit. The wines just keep getting better! ❀ The current winery releases can be sampled and purchased in the tasting room. The beautifully landscaped grounds, reminiscent of the Italian countryside, provide an alluring venue for a picnic of cheeses and charcuteries, also available in the tasting room and a perfect accompaniment to Duchman wines.

13308 FM 150 West • (512) 858-1470 • http://duchmanfamilywinery.com

DRIFTWOOD

SHRIMP DIABLO

Jumbo (16–20 count) shrimp, peeled, deveined, and butterflied

Onion slivers

Slices of seeded fresh jalapeños

Thin-sliced bacon

Salt Lick Dry Rub or your favorite rub

Salt Lick BBQ Sauce or your favorite barbecue sauce

Place an onion sliver and a slice of jalapeño inside each shrimp. Wrap the shrimp in bacon slices and season with dry rub. Place on hot grill and baste with barbecue sauce. Flip and baste again, cooking only until the shrimp turn white throughout. Serve hot, with additional sauce if desired.

(Scott Roberts)

The Salt Lick

Driftwood

Thurman Roberts Sr. and his wife, Hisako, founded this barbecue restaurant in 1969 on the ranch where he was born. Across the road from the ranch is Camp Ben McCullough, a reunion ground for Confederate veterans and their descendants. The Robertses figured that those folks might be potential customers for the family's renowned barbecue recipes. For their opening weekend they bought as much meat as they could afford and sold out. So the next weekend they bought a little more, and the rest, as they say, is history. ❋ In those early years the location of the Salt Lick was considered remote. But that has never stopped folks from making the journey—even though you have to bring your own beer and wine (Hays County is dry) and the restaurant takes cash only! ❋ The Salt Lick has expanded over the years, adding a separate pavilion for weddings and other events. But the original structure, built of stone quarried from the ranch, retains its rustic feel. Just inside the door you'll see one of the few open barbecue pits left in the Hill Country, piled high with brisket, ribs, and sausage. Meals are served family style on long picnic tables and include potato salad, coleslaw, beans, bread, pickles, and onions. On an average weekend the Salt Lick cooks 2,000 briskets alone! ❋ Now operated by the Robertses' son, Scott, the restaurant has won numerous "Best Barbecue" awards and has been featured in dozens of magazines, including *GQ, People,* and *Southern Living.* ❋ Barbecue, sauces and seasonings, and gift merchandise can be ordered through the Web site. Long-term plans for the Salt Lick include vineyards and, eventually, a winery. The dream continues.

18301 FM 1826 • (512) 858-4959 • www.saltlickbbq.com

52

Onion Creek Farm
Dripping Springs

Situated on thirty-six acres of mostly alluvial floodplain on the banks of Onion Creek in Dripping Springs, Onion Creek Farm has been certified by the Texas Department of Agriculture as an organic farm since 1983. ❦ Marianne Simmons, a botanist and former produce manager at Austin's original Whole Foods Market, purchased the farm in 1991 out of a deep love of produce and the business of produce. ❦ When Marianne took over the farm, she sold produce every Saturday morning at a farm stand she established in Dripping Springs. When the grocery giant H-E-B opened its flagship Central Market in Austin, Onion Creek Farm was the store's first direct vendor. She still sells to Central Market as well as to Austin's Wheatsville Co-op. ❦ Over the years, Marianne has transitioned from larger-scale, intensive vegetable production to growing and marketing a wide variety of culinary herbs, par-

ticularly basils, and certain seasonal vegetables, such as tomatoes, squashes, chilies, garlic, and greens. Nearly all the work on the farm is done the old-fashioned way with hoes and knives. All produce is hand-harvested at the peak of ripeness to deliver the fullest flavor and nutrition to the customer.

1611 Creek Road •
(512) 858-1090
• www.ocfarm.com

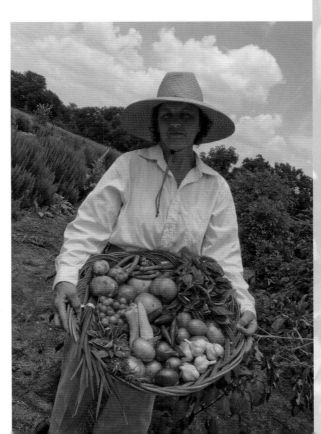

TOMATO AND BASIL SOUP

This soup, which combines three of Onion Creek Farm's products, tastes like the essence of summer itself, with the lusty notes of garlic, the zesty fresh flavor of juicy tomatoes, and the seductive nuances of fresh basil—three of the best things summer has to offer bundled up into one bowl!

Yield: About 3 quarts

9 large garlic cloves, peeled
2½ tablespoons minced basil leaves
2 small to medium onions, coarsely chopped
¼ cup extra-virgin olive oil
2½ quarts chopped garden-fresh Roma
   tomatoes and their juice
½ cup dry vermouth
2¼ teaspoons Oriental chili paste with garlic
1 tablespoon sugar
1½ quarts good-quality chicken stock
Salt to taste
3 cups whipping cream
½ cup grated Reggiano Parmesan cheese

Place steel blade in food processor. With processor running, drop the garlic cloves through the feed tube to mince. Stop the processor and scrape down the sides of the bowl. Add the basil and onions. Process until smooth and well pureed; set aside.

   In a heavy 6-quart soup pot heat the olive oil over medium heat until hot. Add the garlic puree and cook, stirring often, until puree is wilted and transparent, about 5 minutes. Do not allow the mixture to brown. Puree the tomatoes with their liquid. Add the tomato puree to the soup pot and stir to blend well. Cook, stirring often, until the mixture is thickened, about 8 minutes. Stir in the vermouth, chili paste, sugar, and chicken stock. Blend well and add salt to taste. Cover pan and simmer for 30 minutes. Add the whipping cream and cook, covered, for 15 minutes.

   Whisk in the Parmesan cheese, blending well. Simmer an additional 15 minutes. Serve hot.

(Terry Thompson-Anderson)

LAVENDER-INFUSED SANGRIA

Here are two great recipes from Sibby's collection at Onion Creek Kitchens, both paying homage to the bounty of lavender grown in the Hill Country.

Yield: About 1½ quarts

1 large orange, sliced
1 lime, sliced
1 lemon, sliced
Lavender Syrup (see recipe below)
¼ cup good-quality brandy
1 bottle (750 ml) red wine
1 bottle (12-ounce) club soda

Lavender Syrup

1 cup water
1 cup sugar
2 tablespoons dried culinary lavender buds

Make the Lavender Syrup. In a small saucepan, bring water and sugar to a boil and stir until dissolved. Remove from heat and add lavender buds. Cover and allow syrup to stand for 1 hour. Strain into a glass container, cover, and keep refrigerated for up to a few weeks.

In a large glass pitcher, combine the fruit slices. Add the brandy, Lavender Syrup, and wine. Stir to blend well. Refrigerate until well chilled, about 2 hours. When ready to serve, fill wine glasses with ice and fill glasses one-half to two-thirds full of the sangria mixture. Top with desired amount of club soda. Add fruit slices to glasses.

(Onion Creek Kitchens)

Onion Creek Kitchens at Juniper Hills Farm

Dripping Springs

Travis "Sibby" Barrett is a native Texan who operated a Dallas flower company, bakery shop, event-planning business, and restaurant before she moved to the Hill Country and established Juniper Hills Farm. ❋ The farm offers four luxury casitas and two studios for weekend getaways in a scenic, restful spot. A gorgeous infinity-edge pool completes the scene. ❋ But for a truly unforgettable experience, sign up for a class at Sibby's wildly successful Onion Creek Kitchens Cooking School. The classes were originally taught in her well-equipped home kitchen, but in 2010 Sibby built an events center with a state-of-the-art commercial kitchen. The architectural design is a stunning blend of materials with innovative interior accents incorporating Sibby's eclectic silverware collection. The new facility can accommodate private dinners, corporate events, bridal luncheons and rehearsal dinners (but no weddings), as well as vintner dinners featuring area wineries. ❋ In Sibby's popular Random Acts of Cooking classes, students go on a field trip to farmer's markets, olive orchards, artisan cheese makers, and other foodie venues, then return to the classroom to cook a delicious feast from their market finds. She has expanded classes to include a Cooking Live series featuring outside chefs and cookbook authors.

5818 RR 165 • (830) 833-0910 •
www.juniperhillsfarm.com

LAVENDER-ORANGE ICE CREAM

2½ cups whole milk

2½ cups whipping cream

2 vanilla beans

Zest of 1 orange, 1 teaspoon reserved

6 or 7 fresh lavender sprigs, 1 sprig reserved, or substitute 1 tablespoon plus 1 teaspoon dried culinary lavender

6 egg yolks

1 cup sugar

Juice of 1 orange

In a large saucepan combine milk and cream. Split vanilla beans lengthwise. Using a small paring knife, scrape out seeds and add the seeds and pods to the milk mixture. Add the orange zest and lavender sprigs. Bring to a boil over medium heat. Remove from heat and allow to steep for 30 minutes.

Meanwhile, finely chop the remaining lavender sprig and set aside with the reserved 1 teaspoon of orange zest. Combine egg yolks and sugar in bowl of electric mixer. Beat at medium speed until mixture is light lemon-yellow in color and the sugar is completely dissolved. Reheat the milk mixture until very hot but not boiling. Slowly pour about a third of it into the egg yolks, beating constantly. Then pour the milk and egg mixture into the saucepan with the remaining milk. Cook over medium heat, stirring constantly with a wooden spoon, until the custard is thick and coats the back of the spoon. Do not let it boil. Remove the vanilla bean pods and strain the mixture into a large bowl. Add the reserved lavender and orange zest and whisk in the orange juice. Allow mixture to cool to room temperature, stirring occasionally.

Refrigerate until well chilled, or up to two days. When ready to make the ice cream, process in an ice cream freezer according to the manufacturer's instructions. Serve when firm enough to scoop.

(Onion Creek Kitchens)

CILANTRO AND GOAT CHEESE MASHED POTATOES

For a different twist on plain old mashed potatoes, try this variation. Even those who claim to not care for the taste of goat cheese love 'em!

Yield: 4 servings

1 pound small unpeeled new potatoes, quartered

2 tablespoons unsalted butter

1 small onion finely diced (about ½ cup)

4 ounces Pure Luck Texas Plain Chèvre

1 heaping tablespoon minced cilantro

¼ teaspoon freshly ground black pepper

¾ teaspoon sea salt

Place potatoes in a heavy 3-quart saucepan and add cold water to cover. Bring to a full, rolling boil over medium-high heat and cook for 20 minutes, or until potatoes are very soft.

While potatoes are cooking, melt butter in a heavy 8-inch skillet over medium heat. Add onions and sauté, stirring often, until wilted and transparent, about 5 minutes. Remove from heat and set aside.

Drain potatoes in a colander and transfer to a medium bowl. Add the sautéed onions and any residual butter in the skillet, chèvre, cilantro, salt, and pepper. Mash the potatoes with a potato masher, incorporating the other ingredients. Leave them slightly lumpy. Serve hot.

(Terry Thompson-Anderson)

Pure Luck Texas

Dripping Springs

The Pure Luck Farm and Dairy, home of 100 Nubian and Alpine goats and five acres of organic farmland on Barton Creek, produces artisan goat cheese and certified organic culinary herbs. Every aspect of the operation is done by hand with love. ❖ Pure Luck was founded by the late Sara Sweetser Bolton in 1979 on acreage that had been a working tomato farm in the 1930s. She tilled the rich soil and put in a productive vegetable garden to feed her two young daughters, Gitana and Amelia. While caring for a friend's goats, she decided to get a herd of her own and was soon producing goat's milk and cheese. In 1988 Pure Luck was one of the first farms in Texas to apply to the Texas Department of Agriculture for certification as an organic farm. ❖ The first crop grown for sale on the farm was cucumbers, which were eagerly purchased by Whole Foods Market in Austin. The farm was soon growing fresh-cut, organic culinary herbs, which are now harvested twice a week and delivered to local Whole Foods Market and Central Market stores. The cheese production went commercial in 1995. Continuing the labor of love created by their mother, Amelia serves as president of Pure Luck and Gitana as vice-president. The award-winning cheeses are made with the assistance of cheese maker Juana Mora. ❖ As a farmstead operation, Pure Luck uses only milk produced on the premises in making its six distinct types of goat cheese: various seasoned chèvres, feta, Del Cielo (a Camembert-type cheese), Sainte Maure, Hopelessly Bleu, and Claire de Lune (a hard aged cheese). ❖ The cheeses are served in upscale Central Texas restaurants and can also be purchased in Austin at Boggy Creek Farm, Central Market, Farm to Market Grocery, Wheatsville Co-op, and Whole Foods Market as well as at Becker Vineyards near Stonewall and Texas Specialty Cut Flowers in Wimberley. Private tours, which include tastings of the various cheeses, can be arranged at the farm.

3000 Martin Road • (512) 917-2803

• www.purelucktexas.com

Rolling in Thyme & Dough

Dripping Springs

One of the Hill Country's most unique places is Rolling in Thyme & Dough, a bakery and café ensconced in a 100-year-old cottage on a large tree-shaded lot. Few can resist the heavenly smells emanating from the tiny kitchen or the ambiance created by the collection of odd tables and chairs alongside antique sideboards, armoire, pie safe, and hutches filled with tempting goodies. ❧ The cozy eatery was opened in 2005 by two close friends who wanted to create a comfortable place where locals could gather. In 2010 Fabienne Bollom became the sole owner. Belgian-born Fabienne makes all menu items from scratch and offers a marvelous selection of European-style breads and pastries. The café is open for breakfast and lunch. ❧ For breakfast Fabienne offers both classic and innovative egg dishes and egg-filled croissants with additions like fresh pesto and cheese; French toast and handmade waffles; and hot oatmeal, granola, and a selection of yogurts. ❧ The lunch menu features soups, salads, handmade pizzas, a tempting array of sandwiches and wraps, a hearty lasagna, and daily specials, all made from scratch using fresh, local ingredients and organic vegetables from local farmers. Or you can just pick a table, either inside or out in the garden, and enjoy a good cup of coffee, one of the café's specialty coffee drinks, or hot tea. ❧ Bistro Night, on Thursdays, has become a very popular event, featuring live music and a full menu of dazzling dishes that changes each week. From the beginning the café has been deeply involved in the community, which has enthusiastically embraced it in return.

333 U.S. 290 West • (512) 894-0001 • www.thymeand-dough.com

TARTE À LA FRANGIPANE
(Almond Tart)

The almond meal used in the filling for this recipe is made by grinding 8 ounces (2 cups) of sliced, skin-on almonds in the food processor until they are reduced to a fine meal.

Yield: 6 to 8 servings

1 package frozen Pepperidge Farm puff pastry (2 sheets), thawed

Almond Filling
½ pound (2 sticks) butter
1 cup sugar
1 cup almond meal
1 cup all-purpose flour
3 eggs plus 1 egg for egg wash

Glaze
4 ounces apricot preserves
½ cup powdered sugar
1 teaspoon fresh lemon juice
Toasted sliced almonds

Preheat oven to 350 degrees. Set aside one sheet of the puff pastry. Roll out the remaining sheet until very thin. Place the pastry in a 12-inch tart pan, trimming off the edges. Refrigerate.

Make the Almond Filling. In bowl of electric mixer, beat the butter at medium speed until very creamy. Add the sugar and 1 egg, beating to blend well. Add the almond meal and the remaining 2 eggs, one at a time, stopping to scrape down the sides of the bowl after each addition. Beat just to blend, then add the flour, beating until well blended.

Turn the filling out into the chilled pastry, spreading evenly. Using a sharp knife, cut the remaining sheet of puff pastry into strips ½ inch wide. Arrange the strips in a lattice pattern over the top of the filling. Beat the eggs for the egg wash and brush it over the surface of the lattice strips. Bake tart in preheated oven for 35 to 40 minutes, or until filling is set and pastry is golden brown.

While the tart is baking, heat the apricot preserves until very thin. Strain through a fine strainer, stirring to remove all of the jelly; discard the pulpy fruit. When tart is done, brush the preserves over the top. Combine the powdered sugar and lemon juice, blending well. Brush over the top of the apricot glaze, then scatter some sliced almonds over the tart. Allow glaze to set before slicing.

(Rolling in Thyme & Dough)

Alamo Springs General Store and Café

Fredericksburg

The Alamo Springs General Store and Café is definitely off the beaten path—about ten miles southeast of Fredericksburg via the Old San Antonio Road. Look for signs to the Old Tunnel Wildlife Management Area, where three million bats make their home in an abandoned railroad tunnel. ❄ The "Bat Cave," as the tunnel is called, is the main reason why Mike Tangman opened the café. He figured the folks coming to see the bats would be made-to-order customers, as there certainly isn't anywhere else nearby to get a bite to eat! He was right, but his clientele is much larger. Residents from all over the area hang out here, and it's a favorite stop for bicyclists riding the back roads. It's been written up in publications all over the country and memorialized by several film crews. You can even buy t-shirts and tank tops with the café's mantra: "Alamo Springs Café—Where Anybody Is Nobody." ❄

Mike opened the store and café on Memorial Day in 2004. His original concept was to sell upscale deli-style sandwiches and homemade soup in the café, with a burger to satisfy kids. The very first customer to walk in the door ordered the burger and raved about how good it was. So the next customer ordered one too, and the next . . . . At the end of his first week, Mike threw away 80 pounds of gourmet deli meats and ordered 80 pounds of ground chuck. ❄ This is a seriously delicious burger, with awesome hand-cut fries, and it's been named the "Best Burger in Texas" in news articles from coast to coast. You have a choice of great buns—Sourdough Jalapeño-Cheese or Whole Wheat. Mike's burger reigns, although great sandwiches (like Chicken Chipotle), salads, and homemade potato chips are on the menu. ❄ To spend more time managing the store, Mike hired Chef George Fuentes to take over the kitchen and add dinner specials, such as Grilled Quail

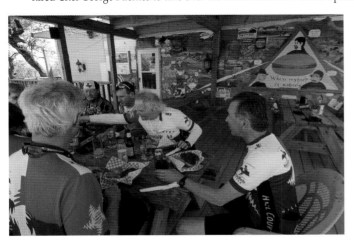

Salad. ❄ This is a fun place. You can drink a brew or two—you'll find your Lone Star as well as plenty of Shiner Bock and Negro Modelo—or enjoy wines by the glass or bottle. There's a front porch and a big deck, offering perfect venues for people-watching.

107 Alamo Road
• **(830) 990-8004**

BLACKENED CENTER-CUT PORK LOIN CHOP

Chef George Fuentes serves this delectable pork chop with a citrus and mango rice studded with toasted almonds and basil.

Yield: 4 servings

4 (8-ounce) center-cut boneless pork loin chops
Your favorite Cajun-style seasoning

Sauce
¾ cup dry white wine
¼ cup honey
¼ cup plus 1 tablespoon Dijon-style mustard
⅔ cup whipping cream
¼ teaspoon salt
¼ teaspoon ground white pepper
1 tablespoon butter

To make the sauce, combine the wine, honey, and mustard in a heavy saucepan and bring to a full boil. Lower heat and cook until the mixture is reduced by half. Stir in the whipping cream and season to taste with salt and white pepper. Simmer for an additional 15 minutes.

While the sauce is simmering, liberally season both side of the pork chops with Cajun seasoning, patting the seasoning into the meat with your fingers. Heat a cast-iron skillet over medium-high heat until very hot. Add the pork chops and cook until an instant-read thermometer inserted into the thickest part of the meat registers 145 degrees. Set aside and keep warm.

Remove sauce from heat and whisk in the butter. Serve the chops topped with a portion of the sauce.

(Alamo Springs General Store and Café)

AUGUST E'S SIGNATURE CRAB STACK AND CROSTINI

Yield: 4 servings

½ pound backfin crabmeat
⅓ cup chopped parsley
½ teaspoon salt
Pinch of black pepper
Juice of 1 lime
Olive oil
1½-inch PVC pipe, cut into four 4-inch lengths (for molds)
3 medium tomatoes, chopped
2 small avocados, chopped
Crostini
Classic Remoulade

Crostini

Half of a baguette, sliced into ¼-inch pieces
Olive oil
Pinch of salt
Parsley

Classic Remoulade

1 cup of mayonnaise
¼ cup chili sauce
2 tablespoons Creole mustard
2 tablespoons extra-virgin olive oil
1 tablespoon Louisiana-style hot sauce, or to taste
2 tablespoons fresh lemon juice
1 teaspoon Worcestershire sauce
4 medium scallions, chopped
2 tablespoons chopped fresh parsley
2 tablespoons chopped dill pickle
1 clove garlic, minced
½ teaspoon chili powder
1 teaspoon salt, or to taste
½ teaspoon ground black pepper
1 teaspoon capers, chopped (optional)

To make the Classic Remoulade, combine all ingredients in work bowl of food processor fitted with steel blade. Process until smooth. Refrigerate until ready to use.

Preheat oven to 350 degrees. Toss baguette slices with olive oil, salt, and parsley. Bake in preheated oven 7 to 10 minutes, or until crisp but not browned.

Combine crabmeat and half the parsley in a medium bowl. Add salt, pepper, and lime juice; mix well. Oil the inside

(continued)

August E's

Fredericksburg

When word spread that a new restaurant by the name of August E's was opening in a rustic log cabin just east of Fredericksburg, the town was abuzz with speculation. "What kind of name is that?" everyone asked. ❧ By the time Dawn and Leu Savanh opened August E's in October of 2004, it was common knowledge that they had also purchased the historic August Eber homestead in nearby Grapetown and named their restaurant in honor of the Eber family's role in area development. Mystery solved. ❧ In 2007 Dawn and Leu were able to purchase a large building in the heart of Fredericksburg's historic district. They converted the interior into a space that wows—the perfect setting for their menu, which they've labeled Nouveau Texas Cuisine. It's an innovative fusion of traditional Texas fare with the foods of Leu's Laos/Thai roots. The total package of August E's, from the décor to the food to the superlative level of service, has added a new dimension of sophistication to dining in Fredericksburg. August E's garnered a Three Diamond rating from AAA, and in 2008 it became only the seventeenth restaurant in the state to make the prestigious DiRoNA list (Distinguished Restaurants of North America). ❧ Dawn began her career in hotel destination management, eventually working for the Anatole Hotel in Dallas. Here she met Leu, a martial arts instructor who had immigrated to the United States when he was fourteen and spoke not a word of English. After discovering that Leu was a fabulous cook, Dawn introduced him to the Anatole's chef, who also saw his potential and brought him into the hotel's kitchens to train as a chef. When Dawn and Leu were ready to try a restaurant of their own, they relocated to an area they had visited often and grown to love. ❧ Leu says the inspiration for his fabulous flavor pairings comes from a creative spot deep inside, adding, "When you first love to cook, the rest comes naturally." His creativity leads to lots of experimenting, always starting with the freshest and best local ingredients he can find. The Savanhs hope to see the day when the Hill Country has a large co-op of local farmers and ranchers growing organic vegetables and free-range animals for area restaurants.

203 E. San Antonio Street • (830) 997-1585 • www.august-es.com

of each length of pipe and stand it upright on a cutting board or plate. Fill a third of the pipe with the crab mixture, then add chopped tomatoes and avocados until the pipe is half full. Repeat with the remaining crab mixture, tomatoes, and avocados; top with the remaining chopped parsley and set aside.

Place the Classic Remoulade in a plastic squeeze bottle. (You may have to cut off a portion of the pointed tip to allow the sauce to pass through.) Squiggle a liberal portion of the sauce across each individual serving plate. Using a small, clean glass bottle, press the crab mixture out of the pipe and onto the center of a serving plate. Arrange 4 to 6 Crostini around each Crab Stack and serve.

Variation: Instead of the remoulade, serve with wasabi aioli, which can be purchased commercially at Whole Foods Market or an Asian market.

(Leu Savanh)

GRILLED JALAPEÑO-STUFFED QUAIL WITH HILL COUNTRY STRAWBERRY-CABERNET GLACÉ AND MESCLUN GREENS WITH WALNUT DRESSING

Mesclun is a salad mix of small, young salad leaves and is found in specialty produce markets and many upscale supermarkets. Although the assortment of greens can vary, the salad mix is generally composed of arugula, dandelion, frisée, mizuma, oak leaf, mâche, radicchio, and sorrel. When selecting mesclun, look for crisp leaves with no sign of wilting.

Yield: 2 servings

½ cup Becker Vineyards cabernet sauvignon
½ cup sugar
1 shallot, peeled and chopped
2 whole cloves
1 teaspoon whole black peppercorns
¼ cup strawberry preserves
4 semi-boneless quail
2 fresh jalapeños, split lengthwise
4 strips of applewood-smoked bacon
Kosher salt and freshly ground black pepper

Mesclun Greens with Walnut Dressing

2 tablespoons walnut oil
¼ cup olive oil
1 tablespoon freshly squeezed lemon juice
2 tablespoons toasted walnut pieces, chopped fine
Kosher salt and freshly ground black pepper
2 cups mesclun greens

Combine the wine, sugar, shallot, cloves, and peppercorns in a medium saucepan over medium-high heat; bring to a boil. Reduce in volume until the wine mixture begins to lightly coat the back of a spoon. Remove from heat and strain while still hot; discard the spices. Add the strawberry preserves to the hot wine mixture and stir until preserves are melted and well mixed; set aside and keep warm.

Preheat gas grill. Place a jalapeño half in the cavity of each quail and wrap quail with a strip of bacon, securing with a toothpick. Season quail with salt and pepper and grill for about 5 minutes per side, turning once, or until the juices from the quail run clear. Transfer quail to a warm platter and remove toothpicks.

Whisk together the walnut oil, olive oil, lemon juice, and walnut pieces; add salt and pepper. Toss the mesclun greens with the walnut dressing.

Place the greens in the center of the platter. Arrange quail around the platter, slightly overlapping the greens. Pour the warm glacé over the quail and serve at once.

(The Cabernet Grill)

The Cabernet Grill—Texas Wine Country Restaurant
Fredericksburg

The Cabernet Grill, originally called the Cotton Gin, has been constantly evolving since its opening in 2001 as part of a lushly landscaped bed and breakfast compound, complete with authentic log cabins. Dating from the mid-1800s, the cabins were found in an area of Kentucky and Tennessee, disassembled, and moved to their present location, where they were painstakingly reassembled with modern amenities and antique furnishings added. The restaurant failed after only six months in operation, and the entire property was placed on the market. ❄ Ross Burtwell fell in love with the place and purchased the entire compound. He received his culinary training at El Centro College in Dallas and had the opportunity to hone his skills under some top-rated chefs in the Westin Hotel chain. The restaurant is definitely a family operation. Ross's wife, Mariana, is the sous chef. The couple's daughter Marissa is the hostess; and son Hunter works the dessert/salad station in the kitchen. ❄

Each dish shows Ross's passion for food as well as his attention to detail. The flavors of the locally sourced menu items are woven together to pair perfectly with Texas wines. In fact, Ross changed his wine list to the first all-Texas wine list in the state, making Cabernet Grill truly a Texas Wine

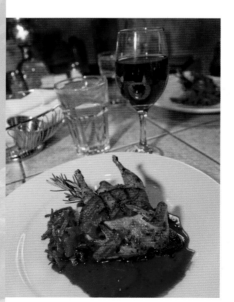

Country restaurant. When he adds a new wine to the list, he trains the waitstaff extensively on pairing each wine with menu offerings, often loading up the entire staff and taking them to the winery to learn about the wines from the winemakers. As a result, diners get expert assistance from the staff in selecting the perfect wine to pair with the dishes they have ordered. The restaurant's bar also serves Texas distilled spirits. Several times a year Ross offers vintner's dinners, creating a sumptuous, multicourse menu featuring the wines of one particular winery or perhaps wines made from grapes grown by the same grape grower but produced at different wineries. These are not-to-be-missed events for wine lovers. You can learn about them by signing up for Ross's newsletter.

Cotton Gin Village • 2805 S. State Hwy. 16 • (830) 990-5734 • www.cottonginlodging.com

Chocolat

Fredericksburg

Master chocolatier Lecia Duke first learned the art of making candy from her grandmother and then attended the famous Wilton School of Cake Decorating and Confectionary Art in Chicago. She started her chocolate career by making corporate logos in chocolate. Some of her early customers were actress Mary Tyler Moore and the Judds of country music fame. ❄ After apprenticing under a Swiss chocolatier to learn how to make chocolates with liquid centers, Lecia founded Quintessential Chocolates in 1984. Her company became the sole U.S. producer of chocolates made with the fine confectionary process known the Liquid Moisture Barrier Technique. Lecia opened Chocolat in 2002. Its present location on Fredericksburg's West Main Street is in the epicenter of the town's popular shopping district. ❄ Lecia fills her chocolates with a wide spectrum of wine-based and nonalcoholic liquid centers in addition to the traditional liqueurs. And even her liqueurs aren't traditional. ❄ The selection of Premium Spirit Chocolates includes morsels filled with chocolate liqueur, crème de menthe, whiskey, Kentucky bourbon, peach schnapps, Russian vodka, Ohranj

(orange), spiced rum, Tennessee whiskey, toffee liqueur, and more. The Crema d'Almendrado Tequila chocolates are notable for having their three distinctive flavors: almond, tequila, and chocolate. In ten years the company has made over 115 different flavors of liquid-center fillings. ❄ In addition to chocolates filled with cabernet, Cognac, tawny port, and raspberry wine, the selection features chocolates made with wines from several private-label producers, including two Texas wineries. ❄ Chocolat also makes handmade European-style truffles, barks, nut clusters, and other fine specialty confections. All candies are made fresh daily on the premises. ❄ If your Hill Country itinerary includes Fredericksburg, be sure to visit Chocolat. You can even watch the chocolates being made!

251 W. Main Street • (830) 990-9382 • www.chocolat-tx.us

Cranky Frank's Barbecue Company

Fredericksburg

Dan and Kala Martin opened Cranky Frank's in 2003. Their son Frank, only a year old at the time, was always cranky, hence the name of their barbecue joint. ✹ But Cranky Frank's is more than a joint. There's a nice dining room in addition to picnic-style seating outdoors, where you can smell the meat slow-cooking over mesquite coals in huge pits. ✹ The most important thing, though, is the excellent barbecue: perfectly smoked brisket with a nice little red smoke ring and pork ribs that fall off the bone with a couple of tugs from the teeth. There is also great sausage, pork roast, and chopped beef with all the requisite sides—potato salad, pinto beans, coleslaw, burger pickles, and chopped onions. Everything's made fresh daily, and it's all good. The Martins make two kinds of barbecue sauce, one from an old German family recipe and another in a traditional style. There are plenty of cold longnecks to savor with your meal. ✹ When you're hankering for some good barbecue while you're in Fredericksburg, stop by Cranky Frank's and step up to the counter to place your order.

**1679 S. Washington Street (U.S. 87 South) •
(830) 997-2353 • www.crankyfranksbbq.com**

65

Der Küchen Laden
Fredericksburg

In search of a microplane or perhaps a kugelhopf pan, a Japanese hand-rolled and folded cobalt steel boning knife, some great coffee beans, an obscure cookbook, or some French porcelain ramekins? You can find them all at Der Küchen Laden (The Kitchen Shop). The store is a mecca for confirmed foodies—and an interesting browse even for those who aren't serious cooks. The great selection includes kitchen towels, potholders, and decorative kitchen accessories as well as those more specialized, hard-to-find items. ❦ Der Küchen Laden first opened in Fredericksburg in 1978 as a very small kitchenwares shop. Husband-and-wife team Jerry and Penny Hughes, who both grew up with a love of cooking, bought the shop in 1993 and in 2000 moved it to its present location, the ground floor of the historic Keidel Memorial Hospital. Penny's grandfather, a physician, had bought the building in the 1930s and turned it into Fredericksburg's first modern hospital after it had been operated as a

retail store. ❦ Jerry's extensive knowledge of fine cookware and kitchen gadgetry as well as his in-store cooking and product demonstrations were loved by customers before he passed away in 2012. His legacy lives on in the shop's various nooks and crannies, which are filled with everything needed in a kitchen. ❦ Penny, a Fredericksburg native who attended Le Cordon Bleu in London, sees the shop as continuing to offer exciting possibilities to cooks at all levels of expertise, empowering them to cook good food at home, as she and Jerry did together. One of the best things about Der Küchen Laden is the knowledgeable staff. If you can describe what you're looking for, they can most likely lead you to it—and show you how to use it!

258 E. Main Street • (830) 997-4937
•www.littlechef.com

Der Lindenbaum

Fredericksburg

Amid the many tourist-oriented German restaurants in Fredericksburg, one in particular is a shining example of a place serving authentic German food. Ingrid Hohmann, a professional chef, opened Der Lindenbaum with a commitment to serving the real deal. She named the restaurant after Germany's beloved linden tree, which grew in front of her family's home in the Eifel Mountains. ❦ A graduate of the prestigious hotel and restaurant school at Maria Laach, Ingrid began her professional career as a *konditormeister*, or pastry chef, making apple strudels, Black Forest cake, and other European pastries. ❦ Der Lindenbaum offers many dishes not commonly found on German restaurant menus in the United States. One of the specialties here is Königsberger Klopse, a fabulous dish of beef and pork meatballs swimming in a delicate caper sauce over egg noodles. Other excellent dishes are Rheinischer Sauerbraten, beef roast marinated for an entire week in a sweet-sour sauce and then slow-roasted until it's fork-tender; Curry Huhn, an amazing curried chicken dish; Gulasch, a spicy beef stew; Schweinekotelett, pork chops in a heavenly mustard sauce . . . the list goes on! Der Lindenbaum's schnitzels are fantastic, as are the German sausages. ❦ You'll find one of the Hill Country's best selections of German beer and wine at Der Lindenbaum—requisite beverages for Ingrid's food! Naturally, you'll want to save room for those sinfully rich German desserts with which she began her culinary career and has honed to perfection over the years. You'll also enjoy the cozy atmosphere of the intimate rock-walled dining room.

312 E. Main Street • (830) 997-9126 •
www.derlindenbaum.com

SERBISCHE BOHNEN SUPPE
(Serbian Bean Soup)

Ingrid serves this comfort-food soup in shallow soup plates. It's easy to prepare, but don't rush it. The secret is in the slow simmering. Serve it with a nice dry German Riesling and some dark bread with real European-style butter. Home-cooked beans and homemade beef stock are preferable, but canned will suffice.

Yield: 4 servings

3 cups Great Northern beans and their cooking liquid
1 large yellow onion, finely chopped
2 green bell peppers, finely chopped
2 red bell peppers, finely chopped
2 cups finely chopped Polish sausage
8 cups beef stock
Tabasco to taste
Salt and freshly ground white pepper to taste
1 tablespoon good-quality soy sauce
2 pork rib bones
2 beef rib bones

Combine all ingredients in a heavy, thick-bottomed 8-quart soup pot over medium heat, stirring to blend well. Simmer the soup slowly for 2 hours, stirring occasionally, or until the beans are quite soft and a thick gravy has formed. Remove the rib bones (great for behind-the-scenes munching in the kitchen). Ladle the soup into shallow bowls and serve hot.

(Der Lindenbaum)

Fredericksburg Brewing Company

Fredericksburg

The Fredericksburg Brewing Company, owned by Richard and Rosemary Estenson, opened in 1994 after the state passed legislation allowing the operation of brewpubs. It is the oldest brewpub in Texas and has been a favorite gathering place since the beginning. The brewery is located in a renovated 1890s limestone building in the heart of the town's busy shopping district. ✾ Before opening the brewery, the Estensons researched brewing equipment

and processes throughout the United States as well as in Germany, Hungary, and the Bohemia region of the Czech Republic. The beers are brewed according to true German traditions, with a current storage capacity of 9,500 gallons. The brewing equipment—huge, shining copper and stainless steel tanks—is in full view of the long bar and dining area. ✾ Brewer Rick Green and

his assistant, Alton Huebner, create five styles of beer in seasonal brews. You can even buy the beers in half-gallon jugs to take home! ✾ At the 2007 Great American Beer Festival in Denver, the largest beer competition in the nation, the brewery's Pioneer Porter received a gold medal in the Brown Porter category. Enchanted Rock Red Ale, a dark English-style ale, won the bronze medal in the Irish-Style Red Ale category. These are two of the brewery's most popular beers.

245 E. Main Street • (830) 997-1646 • www.your-brewery.com

Hilltop Café

Fredericksburg

"If you build it, they will come." Johnny and Brenda Nicholas must have understood that premise long before the popular movie *Field of Dreams* made it a national catchphrase. Back in 1981, when the pair bought the old gas station, grocery store, and beer joint on a lonely hilltop ten miles north of Fredericksburg, they were either very confident or very unaware that location means everything to the success of a restaurant. Whatever their reasoning, Hilltop Café has certainly been a success out there in the middle of absolutely nowhere. ❧ Some of that success may have to do with the fact that Johnny is an internationally known musician and a former member of the wildly popular western swing group Asleep at the Wheel. Or that he plays at the restaurant when he's not away on gigs with his own group, the Texas All Stars. Or it could be the wildly eclectic menu, featuring dishes from Johnny's Greek heritage and Brenda's Cajun roots, plus some Texas favorites like chicken-fried steak and grilled rib eyes priced by the ounce. Johnny credits the word-of-mouth reputation of the food for the success of the place. ❧ Johnny and Brenda try to balance the menu, offering something for everybody and in all price ranges. They use as many local ingredients as possible

and concentrate on fresh, not frozen, products. "You won't find froufrou here," Johnny says, "just great down-home food." Hilltop is also known for its very unique wine list, which offers a wide spectrum of varietals and labels as well as many varietals by the glass. ❧ The Nicholases haven't changed the place: the antique gas pumps still stand sentinel in front, the interior is covered with memorabilia, the wood floors have a patina of wear, and the tables and chairs are an assortment of various styles. It's all part of the café's charm. ❧ A visit to Hilltop Café provides a scenic road trip with a group of adventurous dining friends on Friday and Saturday nights, but be sure to call for reservations at least a week in advance, or you'll find yourself inconveniently located ten miles from Fredericksburg with not the slightest chance of getting dinner! ❧ Hilltop serves one of the Hill Country's best brunches on Sundays, but expect a crowd.

10661 U.S. 87 North • (830) 997-8922 • www.hilltopcafe.com

BAKED CHÈVRE CHEESECAKE

This delicious savory cheesecake featuring goat cheese is a Hilltop Café classic.

Yield: 8 to 10 servings

Crust

- 2½ cups fresh bread crumbs
- 3 tablespoons clarified butter
- 3 tablespoons grated Romano cheese
- 2 garlic cloves, minced
- 2 teaspoons chili powder
- 1 medium pear, peeled, cored, and finely diced

Filling

- 28 ounces cream cheese at room temperature
- 8 ounces soft chèvre (1 cup)
- ⅓ cup half-and-half
- 1 cup sour cream
- 2 garlic cloves, roasted
- ¼ cup finely diced sun-dried tomatoes
- 2 tablespoons minced basil
- 2 tablespoons minced oregano
- 2 tablespoons minced marjoram
- ½ teaspoon kosher salt
- 4 eggs
- Sour cream, rosemary sprigs, and champagne grapes for garnish (optional)

To make the crust, combine all ingredients in work bowl of food processor and process until smooth and well blended. Press the crust into the bottom and sides of a 9-inch spring-form pan. Refrigerate for at least 30 minutes.

Preheat oven to 350 degrees. To make the filling, combine the cream cheese, chèvre, half-and-half, and sour cream in work bowl of food processor. Process until smooth. Add the garlic, sun-dried tomatoes, herbs, and salt. Process just to blend, then add the eggs, one at a time, processing until smooth and creamy after each addition. Pour the filling into the prepared crust and bake in preheated oven for 1 hour, or until firm. Let stand in the oven for 30 minutes after baking.

Refrigerate until well chilled before slicing. Garnish each serving with a dollop of sour cream, a sprig of rosemary, and a small cluster of champagne grapes, if desired.

(Hilltop Café)

Marburger Orchard

Fredericksburg

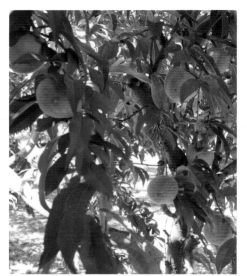

Marburger Orchard, just south of Fredericksburg, is a yearly destination for lots of folks from all over Texas. Come March, they start descending on the vast fields at Marburger to pick their own strawberries. You'll see whole families spaced out over two or three rows at a time. You can pick as many as you've got the fortitude to pick. ❋ After the strawberries have run their course in May, then there are big, succulent blackberries for the picking, followed closely by Fredericksburg peaches, the best in the country! ❋ Marburger Orchard, owned by Gary Marburger, has been a Hill Country tradition since 1978. It's one more farm dedicated to sustainable agriculture and the "eat local" movement. The fruit here isn't shipped across the country to be processed in a warehouse and then loaded onto a truck again to wind up in the supermarket! It goes from the orchard straight to the consumer. ❋ If you just don't feel like walking the fields, Marburger offers prepicked fruits for purchase. You can even taste the different varieties of peaches before you buy. ❋ Marburger provides the heavy cardboard containers for picking, so you can leave your odd assortment of buckets at home. Folks are even encouraged to save the containers from year to year—this saves a lot of trees!

550 Kuhlmann Road • (830) 997-9433 • www.marburgerorchard.com

BRAISED SHORT RIBS

Yield: 4 servings

2 cups red wine, such as cabernet sauvignon

2 pounds meaty short ribs, cut across into 3-inch-long sections and into individual ribs

2 medium red onions, cut into 1-inch dice

2 carrots, cut into 1-inch dice

2 celery stalks, cut into 1-inch dice

5 fresh thyme sprigs

10 fresh parsley sprigs, preferably flat-leaf

Salt and freshly ground black pepper

All-purpose flour

Grapeseed oil

2 cups rich beef or chicken stock

2 tablespoons Dijon mustard

3 tablespoons unsalted butter, cut into small cubes

Cooked grits with jalapeños

Bring the wine to a full boil in a heavy-bottomed saucepan over medium heat; lower heat to a simmer and reduce the wine to 1½ cups. Remove from heat and set aside to cool. Place the ribs in a single layer in a shallow baking pan. Scatter the vegetables between the ribs. Tie the thyme and parsley sprigs into a square of cheesecloth and add to the pan. When the wine has cooled, pour it over the ribs and vegetables. Cover with plastic wrap and refrigerate overnight.

Remove the ribs from the marinade and set aside. Using a slotted spoon, remove the vegetables and herb bundle and set aside, reserving the wine.

Preheat oven to 325 degrees. Pat the ribs dry using absorbent paper towels. Pour ¼ inch of the grapeseed oil into a shallow, heatproof roasting pan large enough to hold the ribs in a single layer; heat over medium-high heat. Season the ribs liberally with salt and pepper on all sides. When the oil is very hot, dust the ribs with flour, coating well and shaking off all excess flour. Add the ribs to the hot oil, searing them until reddish brown and crusty. Turn and sear the other side. Using chef's tongs, quickly remove the ribs and drain on absorbent paper towels. Add the vegetables to the pan, tossing quickly to brown lightly. Add the reserved wine, scraping up the bits of browned meat and vegetables from the bottom. Cook until the wine is reduced to a glaze.

Add the stock and herb bundle; bring to a simmer. Return the ribs to the pan. Remove from heat, cover tightly with foil, and place the pan in the preheated oven. Roast slowly for 3 to 4½ hours, or until a paring knife will easily

(continued)

Navajo Grill
Fredericksburg

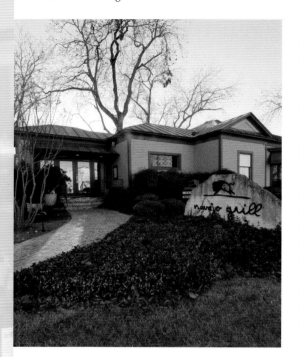

The Navajo Grill is a landmark dining destination for visitors to Fredericksburg as well as a favorite with the locals. The restaurant was opened in 1996 by Fredericksburg chef Steve Howard in a small space on Main Street. It was purchased in 1998 by its present owner, Mike Raymer, a concept development specialist for Walt Disney, National Geographic, and other international companies. He jokingly says that his only prior experience with the food business was that all the men in his family were very good cooks. ❋ After an intensive restaurant boot camp under Chef Howard's tutelage, Mike wondered what he had gotten himself into. But he dug in his heels, learning both the front-of-the-house and back-of-the-house operations by trial and error. "Thankfully, most of the trials worked, and the errors weren't deal-breakers," he says, looking back. ❋ With Mike both at the helm of the kitchen and manager of the operation, the restaurant continued to grow. In 2003 he moved the Navajo Grill to its present location in a free-standing building with an inviting Hill Country ambiance on East Main Street. He added an outdoor courtyard and bar, which is a very popular spot during the many months of pleasant weather in the Hill Country. ❋ In 2006 Mike's son, Josh Raymer, joined the Navajo Grill as executive chef after attending culinary school in Colorado and working his way up in restaurant kitchens in Colorado, California, and Texas. With Josh in charge of the kitchen, the Navajo Grill has become dedicated to sourcing fresh local ingredients to the greatest extent possible. Josh says his philosophy is to create a very ingredient-driven cuisine matched with the best techniques: "We want to surprise and delight our guests, showcasing local cuisine and preparing simple, fresh foods. Texas cuisine is becoming very sophisticated, rooted in the Southwestern cuisine movement but influenced by the proliferation of locally produced foods and Hill Country ethic cooking." Josh's menu changes often, reflecting the seasonality of ingredients. ❋ The Navajo Grill is very much a family affair. From Josh's innovative kitchen to Mike's command of fine service in the dining room, the restaurant garners rave reviews from delighted diners.

803 East Main Street • (830) 990-8289 • www.navajogrill.com

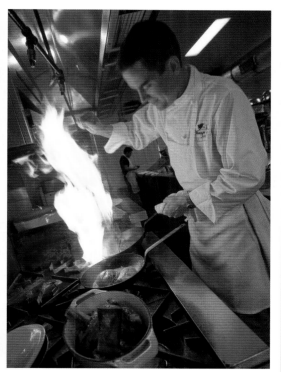

pierce the meat. Remove from oven, allow to cool to room temperature, and refrigerate overnight.

Remove all congealed fat from the surface of the meat and vegetables. Remove the ribs. Remove and discard large pieces of fat from the ribs; set ribs aside. Pour the vegetables, herb bundle, and broth through a fine strainer into a bowl. Press down on the vegetables to extract all the broth. Discard vegetables and herbs; return broth to the pan.

Place the pan over medium-high heat and cook to reduce the broth by half, skimming fat from the surface as needed. Add the mustard, whisking to blend well. Return ribs to the pan and slowly reheat. When the ribs are heated through, remove and set aside; keep warm. Pour the broth into a saucepan over medium-high heat and bring just to a simmer. Remove from heat and add the butter cubes all at once; whisk vigorously to incorporate the butter.

To serve, place a portion of the jalapeño grits in the center of each plate. Top with desired portion of ribs and spoon some of the buttery broth over the ribs and grits. Serve hot.

(Navajo Grill)

FREDERICKSBURG PEACH BREAD PUDDING WITH PEACH AND WHISKEY SAUCE AND CHANTILLY CREAM

Yield: 12 servings

8 ounces white chocolate, cut into small chunks

2 cups half-and-half

¼ pound (1 stick) unsalted butter, softened

½ teaspoon ground cinnamon

10 ounces day-old croissants, cut into ½-inch pieces

3 eggs

¾ cup sugar

7 medium fresh Fredericksburg peaches, peeled and chopped into bite-size pieces (about 3 cups)

½ cup toasted chopped pecans

1 tablespoons vanilla extract

Peach and Whiskey Sauce

½ pound (2 sticks) unsalted butter, softened

1½ cups sugar

2 eggs, beaten until frothy

⅓ cup peach schnapps

3 tablespoons good-quality sour mash whiskey

Chantilly Cream

1 cup whipping cream, well chilled

2 tablespoons sour cream

2 tablespoons powdered sugar

1 tablespoon vanilla extract

Preheat oven to 350 degrees. Butter a 13-by-9-inch baking dish; set aside. In a 2-quart saucepan combine the white chocolate, half-and-half, butter, and cinnamon. Cook over medium-low heat until smooth, stirring often. Remove from heat and set aside. Place croissant pieces in a large bowl and add the white chocolate mixture, blending well and breaking up the croissants. In bowl of electric mixer, combine the eggs and sugar; beat at medium speed until thickened, about 7 minutes. Add the peaches, pecans, and vanilla; beat just to blend. Fold the egg mixture into the croissant mixture, blending well. Turn out into prepared baking dish and bake in preheated oven for 45 to 55 minutes, or until a knife inserted in center comes out clean. Set aside and keep warm.

(continued)

Studebaker Farm

Fredericksburg

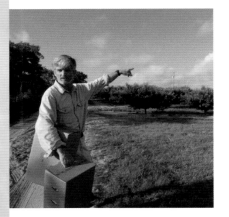

Russell Studebaker is an eighth-generation descendant of Studebakers who came to America from Solingen, Germany, in 1736 and settled in the Midwest. In the 1930s, Russ's paternal grandfather traded his farm in Missouri for land in the Rio Grande Valley. His maternal grandfather, a Swede, had moved to the region in 1913 and was one of the pioneers in developing Rio Grande Valley agriculture. Both farms remain prominent Valley farms, run by Studebaker cousins. ❧ Although Russ's father gave up farming during the long drought of the 1950s, he kept a small cattle herd and loved to plant fruit trees. So from an early age Russ knew the basics of growing fruit. ❧ In 1992 Russ and his wife, Lori, bought land east of Fredericksburg in the community of Blumenthal. Except for a twenty-five-acre orchard, the property was pretty much grown up in mesquite and cedar. The Studebakers cleared and leveled the land, planted cover crops to rebuild the soil, and built a home as well as a farm stand for selling the farm's peaches. ❧ Russ manages the orchard and the harvest, while Lori runs the retail end of the operation. They've not only expanded the orchard on their land but also leased other land, increasing their productive acreage to sixty acres with around 8,000 trees. ❧ The Studebakers enjoy the farming lifestyle, and their children have grown up working alongside Russ and

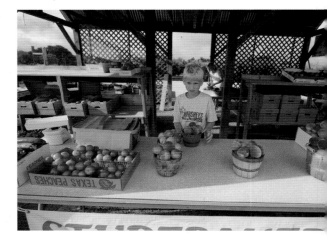

Lori to make the farm a success. ❧ Studebaker Farm has repeat customers from all over the state who come here to buy strawberries, blackberries, peaches, and plums. Seasonal produce is also available. Many customers bring the Studebakers jars of preserves they've made from the farm's peaches. Kids come to see Rosebud, the family dog who goes to the fruit stand with Lori every day.

9405 U.S. 290 East • (830) 990-1109 • www.texaspeaches.com/studebaker

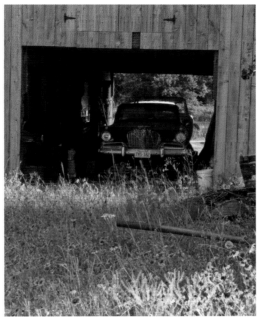

Make the Peach and Whiskey Sauce. Cream butter and sugar in bowl of electric mixer until very light and fluffy, about 7 minutes. Transfer to the top of a double boiler over simmering water. Cook for 20 minutes, whisking often, until the mixture is silky smooth and comes away from the side of the pan when whisked. Whisk ½ cup of the hot butter mixture into the beaten eggs, then another ¼ cup. Whisk the egg mixture slowly into the remaining butter mixture over the heat. Cook until thickened, about 4 to 5 minutes, whisking constantly. Whisk in the schnapps and whiskey and blend. Keep warm over low heat.

Make the Chantilly Cream by combining all ingredients in bowl of electric mixer. Beat at medium speed until the mixture forms loose, floppy peaks. Cover tightly with plastic wrap and refrigerate until ready to serve.

To serve, slice the warm pudding into squares. Ladle a portion of the Peach and Whiskey Sauce into each serving bowl and set a square of pudding in the center. Top with a large dollop of Chantilly Cream.

(Terry Thompson-Anderson)

POW OYSTERS WITH SRIRACHA AIOLI

Yield: 6 servings

Canola oil for deep frying

4 cups all-purpose flour, blended with 1 teaspoon
    cayenne pepper, 1 teaspoon paprika,
    1 tablespoon onion powder, and 1 tablespoon
    granulated garlic

2½ cups club soda or other sparkling water

2 dozen freshly shucked oysters

Mixed salad greens

Your favorite vinaigrette dressing

Sriracha Aioli (see recipe below)

Sweet soy sauce

Fresh snipped chives, toasted sesame seeds, and
    salt and pepper

Sriracha Aioli

1 cup real mayonnaise

1 to 3 tablespoons Sriracha sauce, or to taste

1 teaspoon sambal oleck (spicy chili garlic paste)

Salt

1 garlic clove, peeled and minced using a
    microplane

Heat the oil to 360 degrees. Place 2 cups of the seasoned flour in a large bowl. Add the club soda and whisk until smooth. Place the remaining 2 cups of flour in a separate bowl. Dip each oyster completely in the wet flour mixture, then in the dry flour. Gently drop them in the hot oil, taking care not to crowd them. Fry in batches for 2 to 3 minutes, then remove with a slotted spoon and drain on a wire rack set over a baking sheet.

To make the Siracha Aioli, combine all ingredients and whisk to blend.

Toss the mixed greens with the vinaigrette and place a portion on each serving plate. Top each serving with 4 fried oysters and drizzle with the Sirachi Aioli and sweet soy sauce. Garnish with the chives, sesame seeds, and salt and pepper. Serve at once.

(The Sunset Grill)

The Sunset Grill

Fredericksburg

When Angela Mancino and Jimmy Ehrlich opened the Sunset Grill in the fall of 2010, their timing was perfect. With its heavy tourism, Fredericksburg was in need of a restaurant offering a full, upscale breakfast and a wide variety of lunch dishes plus a Sunday brunch. The Sunset Grill was an instant hit with both locals and visitors. It was a something-for-everyone kind of place with a bright and colorful interior, delicious food, courteous service, and affordable prices. 🌸 Jimmy left the business in 2011, but Angela's passion for cooking keeps diners coming back often. "Opening the restaurant was literally a trial by fire," she says, and learning how to use professional restaurant equipment was one of the most daunting challenges. "I'd worked in a lot of food and wine operations. I would watch the chefs, soaking up how they prepared a particular dish, then go home and duplicate the flavors. It was how I taught myself to cook." Angela created the menu and, before she found a full staff, worked all of the stations in the restaurant. To get the word out when the Sunset Grill first opened, Angela would leave her menus with shop owners on Fredericksburg's busy Main Street, lodging establishments, and bed and breakfast operations. The Sunday brunch was a huge success, as no other restaurant in town was offering a real Sunday brunch at the time. 🌸 The Sunset Grill is a very popular lunch destination, too. The menu boasts an entire page of burgers of every description, sandwiches piled high with

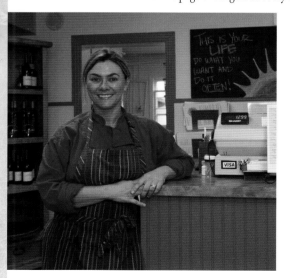

meats and veggies on artisan breads, unique and delicious soups, gargantuan salads with house-made dressings, and daily hot lunches, always including a pasta dish. The restaurant has a small but well-thought-out wine list with offerings by the glass or bottle, along with domestic and imported beer. On Thursday afternoons the Sunset Grill's signature lamb sliders and sometimes its pulled pork and beef sliders can be purchased at the popular Fredericksburg Farmer's Market.

**902 S. Adams Street • (830) 997-5904 •
www.sunsetgrilltx.com**

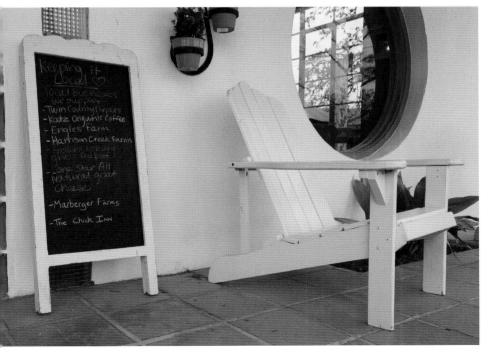

Keeping it
Local
Local Businesses
we support
- Twin County Dairies
- Katz Organic Coffee
- Engles Farm
- Harrison Creek Farms
- Fredricksburg
  Grass Fed beef
- Lone Star All
  Natural goat
  cheese
- Marberger Farms
- The Chick Inn

Cranberry   chocolate Chip
Oatmeal cookies walnut cookies
$2.00 $2.5

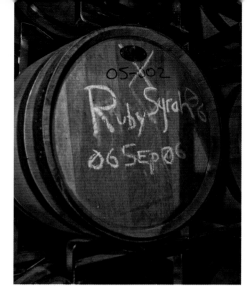

Torre di Pietra Winery

Fredericksburg

Torre di Pietra Winery was founded by Ken and Jenise Maxwell in 2003. After an eight-month search, they found just the right piece of property, fifty acres with highway frontage. ❧ Their consultants suggested they plant French American grapes with a resistance to Pierce's disease—black Spanish (Lenoir) and blanc du bois grapes. They also planted a block of American hybrid Norton grapes. They have been pleased with the reception to the wines they produce from these grapes, which have won many awards. ❧ Before purchasing the winery property, the Maxwells had planted a vineyard in northwestern Gillespie County, near Doss, with vitis vinifera vines—zinfandel, primitivo, petite syrah, cabernet sauvignon, malbec, and muscat canelli. Torre di Pietra was the first winery in Texas to plant petite syrah, and it has proven to be one of their best wines. The winery purchases sangiovese fruit from Anchor Oaks Vineyards near Blanco. ❧ Ken's grandfather and father taught him how to make wine. When he was a young boy, he helped his family pick mustang grapes and make wine in the barn. Torre di Pietra is also a family operation. The Maxwells knew that starting a winery would be hard work but told the children that if they helped to make it a success, it would always be there for them. Ben, the oldest son, manages the Doss vineyard and contributes to other aspects of the business. You'll probably see some of the kids if you visit the winery on a Saturday.

10915 E. U.S. Hwy. 290 • (830) 644-2819 • www.texashillcountrywine.com

Vogel Orchard

Fredericksburg

The Vogel peach lineage goes back to the early 1900s when Armand Vogel planted a few peach trees and sold peaches and eggs under a shade tree to passersby on the road between Stonewall and Fredericksburg. ❧ Armand's son, George, and his wife, Nelda, planted their first orchard in 1953. From just 200 trees that orchard has now grown to over 2,800 trees. In 1972 the Vogels opened a roadside market ten miles east of Fredericksburg near the location where Armand used to sell under that shade tree. The Vogels' youngest son, Jamey, and his wife, Terri, moved back to Fredericksburg in 1998 to help run the family business. ❧ Vogel Orchard continues to offer much

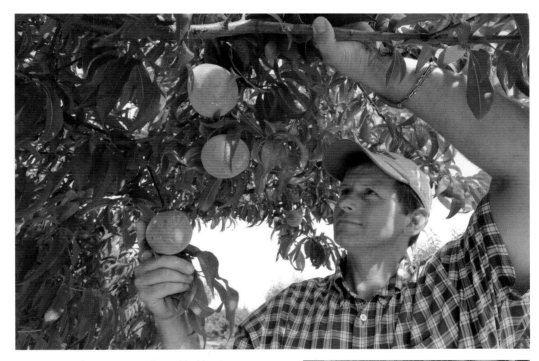

of the same produce that it has for many years—peaches, tomatoes, plums, blackberries, watermelons, cantaloupes, and other vegetables. In addition the roadside market sells homemade peach cobbler, peach ice cream, peach preserves, peach butter, plum jelly, and fig, blackberry, and pear preserves. ❧ Seventeen varieties of peaches are usually available, beginning around the middle of May with Starlite White clingstone peaches. The first freestone variety, Tex Royal, is usually ripe toward the end of May. Plums are harvested in mid-May. The Vogels grow Methley plums, a small

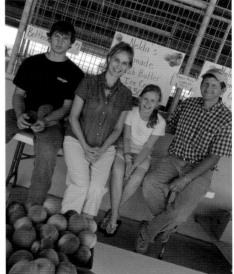

purple-red plum that's sweet as honey. They're so small that at first the Vogels had trouble selling them, so they'd just hand out a few to folks. One taste and they were hooked!

12862 U.S. 290 East • (830) 644-2404 • www.vogelorchard.com

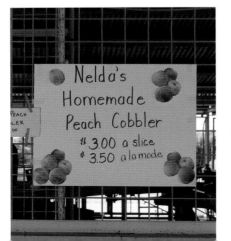

Nelda's Homemade Peach Cobbler $3.00 a slice $3.50 a la mode

GRAPE TOMATO PICO DE GALLO

This very different pico de gallo uses the chiltepin (or chilipitín), commonly known as the bird pepper, the only wild pepper in Texas. In fact, the chiltepin is officially designated as the Texas state native pepper. It's a tiny, volatile chili with a heat level of 8 on a scale of 10; however, the heat dissipates very quickly in the mouth and the resulting taste is quite nice. If you wish to make this condiment ahead of time, don't add the salt until ready to serve.

Yield: About 2½ cups

1 pint grape tomatoes, quartered
⅔ cup chopped cilantro
6 green onions and tops, sliced thin
6 chiltepins, minced, including seeds
Juice of 1 lime
Salt to taste

Combine all ingredients in a bowl and toss to blend well. Refrigerate in a tightly covered container until ready to serve. Serve with homemade tortilla chips or use as a condiment.

(Terry Thompson-Anderson)

Wildseed Farms

Fredericksburg

Wildseed Farms is a very unique place. Founded in 1983 by John and Marilyn Thomas, the farm has become a wildly popular destination for visitors to Fredericksburg from all over the world. ❧ The 200-acre farm grows wildflowers to produce seeds for over eighty varieties of wildflowers. John pioneered the practice of planting wildflowers in rows on large acreage, and today it's the nation's largest working wildflower farm. ❧ Fields of riotous color erupt at the farm when the wildflowers bloom from March through October. Visitors can explore walking trails through the blooming fields or pick their own wildflowers in specially designated areas. A popular attraction is the Butterfly Haus, a special exhibit of 250 species of live butterflies. ❧ The Market Center sells a vast array of wildflower seeds for all parts of the country in packets of individual species as well as mixes. The seeds are also sold through the Web site and a

mail-order catalog. The Brew-Bonnet Biergarten, located in the Market Center, is a delightful place to enjoy a glass or bottle of Texas wine or beer with some vittles from the deli and to browse the vast selection of Texas food products available. ❧ Since 2007, Wildseed Farms has hosted an annual Gourmet Chili Pepper and Salsa Festival, which features seminars on all aspects of chili cultivation and chili culture. Dozens of varieties of chili plants are for sale, including some that are usually hard to find. ❧ Wildseed Farms is also a great source for garden plants—tomatoes, other vegetables, and herbs. You can find some of the more exotic herbs in addition to the familiar ones like dill and basil. Best of all, the helpful and knowledgeable staff is on hand to give pointers on how to best grow and care for the plants they sell.

425 Wildflower Hills (off U.S. 290) • (800) 848-0078 • www.wildseedfarms.com

CHOCOLATE CAYENNE CAKE

Yield: One 9-inch two-layer cake

2 cups sugar
½ cup cocoa powder
2 cups all-purpose flour
2 teaspoons baking soda
1 teaspoon baking powder
½ teaspoon red (cayenne) pepper
1 cup vegetable oil
1 cup buttermilk
1 cup water
2 teaspoons vanilla extract
2 eggs, beaten
Cream cheese frosting with anise (your favorite
   recipe with 1 teaspoon toasted and crushed
   anise seeds)

Chocolate Ganache

1½ cups bittersweet chocolate chips
3 tablespoons unsalted butter
2 tablespoons whipping cream

Preheat oven to 350 degrees. Generously grease two
9-inch cake pans and set aside.
    Combine the sugar, cocoa, flour, baking soda,
baking powder, and cayenne, stirring to blend well. In
a separate bowl, combine the vegetable oil, buttermilk,
water, vanilla extract, and beaten eggs. Add the wet
ingredients to the dry ingredients, beating to blend well.
Divide the batter between the prepared cake pans; bake
in preheated oven for 30 minutes, or until a toothpick
inserted in the center of the cakes comes out clean.
Remove from oven and cool in pans on wire racks for 10
minutes. Turn the layers out onto the rack, allow to cool
completely, and refrigerate until chilled.
    To make the Chocolate Ganache, melt the choco-
late chips and butter in a double boiler over simmering
water; stir until smooth. Add the cream slowly, stirring
until smooth and spreadable.
    To assemble the cake, place one layer on a serving
plate and spread with the cream cheese frosting all the
way to the edge. Place the second layer on top of the
icing. Frost the top and sides of the cake with the Chocolate Ganache. Allow the ganache to set before slicing.

(Elaine's Table)

Elaine's Table

Hunt

The charming limestone building that houses Elaine's
Table was built in the late 1930s as a restaurant catering to summer residents, the families of campers, and
hunters in the winter months. Although it's undergone
a number of renovations, it's been used as a restaurant
for most of its history. ❋ The present incarnation of
the space offers an inviting Hill Country ambiance,
with its limestone interior walls and Mexican tile floors.
There's a fabulous view of the gracefully flowing
Guadalupe River from the back dining area. The large
fireplace in the main dining room offers a cheery glow
during the winter months. ❋ Elaine Bicknell opened
Elaine's Table in 1998, and soon her husband, Bruce,
joined Elaine in operating the restaurant. The community support was evident from the beginning, and the
restaurant quickly became a favorite meeting place for
local residents, especially on Wednesday nights, when
all the tables are grouped together for Family Night.
Huge platters of all manner of goodies are placed in

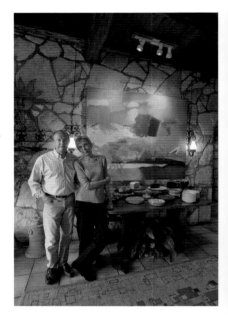

the center of the tables, family-style. ❋ The regular
menu offers a variety of appetizers, soups, salads, and
entrées from seafood to steaks, pork, pasta, chicken,
and a very good chicken-fried steak made with sirloin.
The dessert table offers a tempting array of cobblers,
cakes, pies, and crème brûlée. ❋ During the summer
the restaurant is packed on the drop-off and pick-up
weekends for the large summer camp industry in the
area. Elaine's is also the "launching spot" (and ending
celebratory point) for the annual Hunt Sweet Potato
Queens Parade in February, a private event. The Bick-
nells say that their favorite thing about the restaurant is
their great customers.

**1621 State Hwy. 39 • (830) 238-4484
• www.elainestable.com**

Broken Arrow Ranch

Ingram

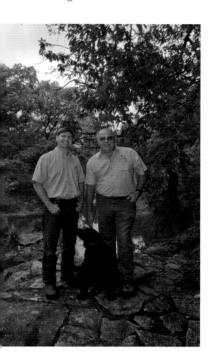

Broken Arrow Ranch, suppliers of free-range, field-harvested wild game, was founded in 1983 by Mike Hughes and his wife, Elizabeth. On a vacation abroad the Hugheses had noticed that venison and other wild game meats were common on menus in European restaurants but almost nonexistent in American restaurants. At the same time, exotic deer species imported by Texas ranchers for hunting purposes were overgrazing Hill Country ranchlands, requiring active population management to maintain the sustainability of both the herd and the land. The Hugheses established Broken Arrow Ranch to provide high-quality wild game meats to the restaurant industry. ❦ Broken Arrow Ranch is the nation's only supplier of truly wild venison. The exotic species harvested by Broken Arrow range free on over 100 Texas ranches that total about one million acres. This land provides native vegetation for browse and gives the meat the complex natural flavors not found in that of farm-raised animals. The animals are range-harvested with techniques that reduce stress to the animal and produce the highest meat quality possible. Working closely with government inspection agencies, Mike developed a portable, trailer-mounted processing facility so that an animal can be processed quickly after being harvested. ❦ In 2005 Mike turned the reins over to his son Chris, who had already learned the business by doing product demonstrations at trade shows, hosting chef retreats at the family's ranch in Ingram, and taking physical inventory counts. ❦ The majority of Broken Arrow's products are sold directly to chefs and restaurants nationwide, but consumers can purchase cuts of venison, antelope, and wild boar for home use through the company's Web site. Eating wild game makes sense with today's health concerns. Broken Arrow's venison and antelope meat averages one-third the calories of beef, one-eighth the fat content of beef, and is lower in cholesterol than a skinless chicken breast!

3296 Junction Hwy. (State Hwy. 27) • (800) 962-4263 •
www.brokenarrowranch.com

SAVORY VENISON STEW

The cooks at the ranch perfected this recipe in the course of feeding the annual hunting camp crowd.

Yield: 8 servings

- 2 pounds Broken Arrow Ranch venison stew meat, cut into bite-size pieces
- 2 bay leaves
- 1½ tablespoons mixed pickling spices, securely wrapped in cheesecloth and tied with kitchen twine
- 2 medium onions, coarsely chopped (2 cups)
- ¼ teaspoon granulated garlic
- ½ teaspoon ground black pepper
- 4 carrots, cut into ½-inch dice
- 4 celery stalks, cut into ½-inch dice
- 4 red potatoes, cut into ½-inch dice
- 4 chicken bouillon cubes
- 1 quart water
- 2 teaspoons red wine vinegar
- 2 cans (8-ounce) tomato sauce

Spray a heavy Dutch oven with nonstick vegetable spray and quickly brown the meat on all sides. Add all remaining ingredients, cover, and simmer over medium heat for about 1½ hours, or until venison is tender and vegetables are cooked. Remove and discard the cheesecloth bag before serving.

(Broken Arrow Ranch)

INGRAM

Hummingbird Farms

Johnson City

Hummingbird Farms, nestled in the serene countryside west of Johnson City, is owned and operated by Jack and Debi Williams. The Williamses planted their first lavender field at Hummingbird Farms in 2003 after they had spent several years researching which types of lavender would be best for the optimal production of essential oil. The Williamses settled on *Lavendula angustifolia*, known variously as common lavender, English lavender, or true lavender. ❀ Hummingbird Farms produces high-quality bath and body products, using only lavender oil, aloe, and other pure ingredients grown in Texas, with no added water or artificial fragrances. The Williamses developed their own formulas for the products, which are available at gift shops and other specialty stores throughout Central Texas or via the Hummingbird Farms Web site. ❀ Hummingbird Farms is open to visitors during the lavender season from the end of May to the end of June and offers cut-your-own lavender.

9430 U.S. 290 West • (830) 868-7862 • www.hummingbirdlavender.com

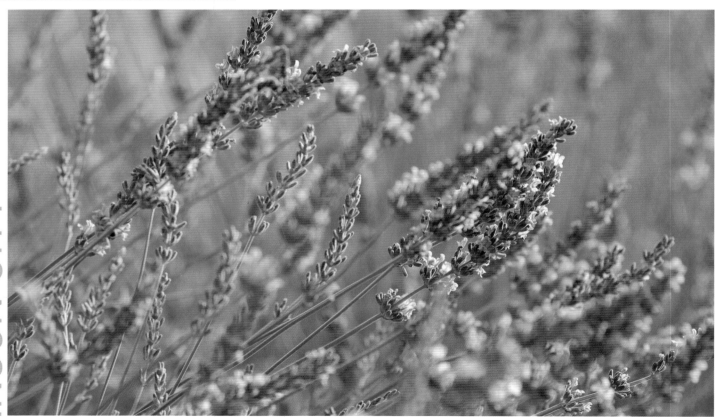

JOHNSON CITY

Pecan Street Brewing

Johnson City

After running a successful blending and packaging business in Houston, Tim and Patty Elliott decided to return to the Hill Country and open a brewpub featuring artisanal beers. The pair purchased the old Blanco County Supply building, an iconic structure across from the courthouse, and gave it new life, repurposing many of the materials. The tin ceiling came from an old church in Johnson City. Pecan Street Brewing opened on June 25, 2011. ❉ The Elliotts brought in their son, Sean, as an equity partner and as the brewer. During the three years that his parents worked on renovating the building and installing a mill where they grind their own grains for their beers, Sean honed his skills as a craft brewer at Old World–style breweries in Europe and in Colorado. He wrote the "recipes" for a wide variety of tantalizing beers in many styles and changes the offerings seasonally. The beers are named after hardware items as well as the local surroundings, such as Screw Loose Blonde, Ten Penny Ale, County Jail Pale Ale, and others. ❉ Pecan Street Brewing also offers a full menu of beer-friendly foods—real brick-oven pizzas, a wide selection of innovative salads, and several types of burgers, including lamb and fish burgers. There's also a nifty selection of dinner plates as well as weekly specials. ❉ The music room has a good-size dance floor, and an outdoor beer garden features live bands every weekend. It's the place to enjoy a frosty mug of excellent beer brewed on-site, savor a satisfying meal, and dance to your heart's content. The dominos and pool tables have made it a popular gathering place with the locals.

106 E. Pecan Drive • (830) 868-2500 • www.pecanstreet-brewing.com

Texas Hills Vineyard

Johnson City

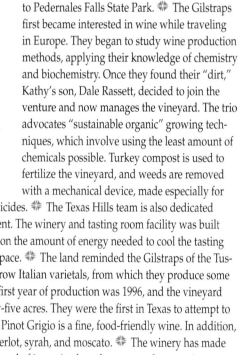

Following in the footsteps of many other entrepreneurs who have given up lucrative professions to move to the Texas Hill Country and "do something different," pharmacists Gary and Kathy Gilstrap sold their successful drugstore in Kansas and headed to the Johnson City area. They were looking for just the right vineyard land, which they found east of town on the road to Pedernales Falls State Park. ❦ The Gilstraps first became interested in wine while traveling in Europe. They began to study wine production methods, applying their knowledge of chemistry and biochemistry. Once they found their "dirt," Kathy's son, Dale Rassett, decided to join the venture and now manages the vineyard. The trio advocates "sustainable organic" growing techniques, which involve using the least amount of chemicals possible. Turkey compost is used to fertilize the vineyard, and weeds are removed with a mechanical device, made especially for organic vineyard cultivation, rather than herbicides. ❦ The Texas Hills team is also dedicated to looking out for the Hill Country environment. The winery and tasting room facility was built using the rammed-earth method to cut down on the amount of energy needed to cool the tasting room—and to make it a very quiet and cozy space. ❦ The land reminded the Gilstraps of the Tuscan countryside, so they initially decided to grow Italian varietals, from which they produce some very noteworthy, award-winning wines. The first year of production was 1996, and the vineyard has grown from twelve acres of vines to thirty-five acres. They were the first in Texas to attempt to grow pinot grigio, and Texas Hills Vineyard's Pinot Grigio is a fine, food-friendly wine. In addition, they grow sangiovese, cabernet sauvignon, merlot, syrah, and moscato. ❦ The winery has made a name for itself on restaurant menus with several of its varietals and two great dessert wines, Moscato and Orange Moscato, plus a ruby port–style wine named Rubino—fabulous with anything chocolate or just for sipping. Texas Hills Vineyard's premium Cabernet Sauvignon, Kick Butt Cab, is two-fisted and full-bodied, a must-have accompaniment to those cowboy rib eyes that we love so dearly in the Hill Country!

878 RR 2766 • (830) 868-2321 • www.texashillsvineyard.com

SPANISH CHOCOLATE TAPAS

Yield: 2 servings

2 slices panini bread, cut diagonally into four pieces
Texas olive oil
Sugar
Dark chocolate squares, broken in 1-inch pieces
Cayenne pepper
Fresh mint leaves, minced
Pecan praline ice cream

Brush the bread with olive oil and sprinkle with sugar. Bake in convection oven at 500 degrees for about 4 minutes or until edges are browned and the sugar is caramelized. Remove and place a piece of chocolate on each piece of panini. Return to oven for about 1 minute or until chocolate is melted.

Using a small spatula, spread the chocolate close to the edges of the bread. Shake a small amount of sugar on top and then tap a shaker of cayenne lightly over each piece. Scatter the mint on each piece. Serve with two tiny scoops of the ice cream. Garnish plate or tray with a sprig of fresh mint.

(Junction Rivers Winery)

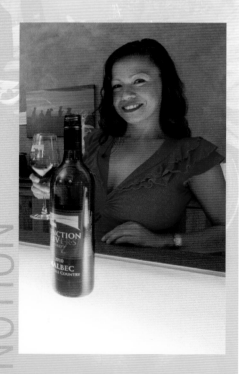

Junction Rivers Winery

Junction

Dr. Joe King and his wife, Jeanie Brosius King, opened Junction Rivers Winery in November of 2011 as a gathering place for both local residents and the town's many tourists. It was the realization of a thirty-year dream. To develop his wine program, Joe hired award-winning winemaking consultant Don Pullum. The wines, made from native hybrid grapes and other Texas-grown varietals, have been an instant hit at the winery's tasting room. ❄ When designing the winery, the Kings included a bistro kitchen so that visitors could linger over their wine while enjoying a selection of food offerings. The covered patio is a perfect place for an al fresco wine and food experience whereas the interior space is finished in soothing Tuscan colors accented with rustic Texas touches of cedar and pine woodwork. From the large tasting room window, visitors can view the production facility where wines are being crafted. The tasting bar is lighted from below, allowing tasters to candle the wines for color and clarity. And the wines are served in etched titanium crystal wineglasses that are large enough for real swirling. ❄ The bistro menu offers cheese and charcuterie boards with assorted house-made spreads and artisan breads as well as toasted flatbread-style pizza, a crostini plate, and desserts. In addition to their wines, the Kings have created "wine-a-ritas," frozen sangria, and frozen lemon bellinis made from their wines. ❄ The most unique feature at the winery is Yappy Hour. Relax and enjoy your food and wine while your furry friend frolics in the outdoor dog park, which you can view on closed-circuit television. If you're a Facebook fan, there's a live Facebook page on a big screen in the tasting room; you can log on, "friend" the winery, and see your wall pictures appear! ❄ The Kings are committed not only to creating fine wines but also to protecting the planet. Junction Rivers Winery was constructed of structurally insulated panels (SIP) to reduce its carbon footprint of energy consumption. There is an outdoor rainwater collection system for watering the grounds, and solar panels and wind turbines will be added in the near future.

210 N. 6th Street • (325) 446-2600 •
www.junctionriverswinery.com

Rails—A Café at the Depot

Kerrville

Does the concept of healthy food that tastes really good sound like an oxymoron? Rails has proven that it can be done. ❧ Owners Melissa Southern and John Hagerla opened the popular café in 2003. Melissa, a registered dietician, was tired of unappealing, tasteless hospital food. She wanted to open a restaurant serving healthy fare that was also delicious. ❧ The café is located in the old depot of the San Antonio & Aransas Pass Railway. Built in 1915, the depot was used until 1970, when the railroad line was abandoned. In renovating the building, Melissa and John created a friendly, laid-back kind of place, not stuffy and upscale. The interior is accessorized with an interesting collection of old railroad memorabilia. The restoration was named Best

Rehabilitation Project in 2004 by the Texas Downtown Association. ❧ Melissa's menu is a delight, offering something for the customer's every mood. There's a large selection of appetizers, some great sandwiches (including an Axis Deer Burger and Grilled Italian Panini), and a variety of salads, full entrées, and daily dinner specials, including a great Pork Shank Osso Buco. Open for lunch and dinner, Rails has a nice wine list, with most of the selections offered by the glass. ❧ Rails has won accolades from *Frommer's San Antonio and Austin* ("Some of the best food in the Hill Country") and the *San Antonio Express-News* ("A small gem polished with local flavor and a bit of history"). And remember, it's all healthy!

615 E. Schreiner Street • (830) 257-3877 • www.railscafe.com

SEARED DUCK BREAST WITH HILL COUNTRY PEACH AND GINGER SAUCE

Yield: 4 servings

4 tablespoons olive oil
1 cup chopped shallots
½ cup sugar
¾ cup low-sodium soy sauce
1½ cups dry red wine
¼ cup balsamic vinegar
2½ tablespoons grated fresh ginger
1½ teaspoons ground cinnamon
½ teaspoon freshly ground black pepper
4 skinless, boneless duck breast halves
3 fresh Hill Country peaches, peeled and chopped

In a heavy 12-inch skillet heat 2 tablespoons of the olive oil over medium heat. Add the shallots and sugar, sautéing until shallots are golden brown. Add the soy sauce, red wine, balsamic vinegar, ginger, cinnamon, and black pepper, stirring to blend well. Cook over low heat for 2 minutes. Cool and reserve 1 cup of the sauce for marinade. Place the duck breasts in a single layer in a Pyrex baking dish. Pour the reserved 1 cup of sauce over the breasts, cover, and refrigerate for 2 hours. Turn occasionally.

Remove duck from marinade and pat dry with absorbent paper towels. Coat the duck breasts with olive oil and season with salt. Heat the remaining 2 tablespoons of oil in a heavy 12-inch skillet over medium-high heat until the oil begins to smoke. Add the duck breast halves and cook 3 minutes on each side, or until golden brown. Remove to a platter and keep warm.

In a heavy medium saucepan, boil the remaining sauce until reduced by half, about 5 minutes. Add peaches and stir until heated through. Pour the sauce over the duck breasts and serve at once.

(Rails—A Café at the Depot)

KERRVILLE

CHOCOLATE AND GOAT CHEESE CRÈME BRÛLÉE

The plain soft chèvre made by Bradley Goat Farms is outstanding in this recipe, which combines the tangy, earthy goat cheese with the best features of chocolate—for an over-the-top delicious dessert. Even goat-cheese haters love it.

Yield: Six 6-ounce ramekins

⅓ cup light brown sugar

2¼ cups whipping cream

4½ tablespoons sugar

3 ounces bittersweet chocolate

2 tablespoons Dutch-process cocoa

4 egg yolks

2½ teaspoons vanilla extract

7½ ounces goat cheese at room temperature

Preheat oven to 250 degrees. Spread the brown sugar in a thin layer on a baking sheet and place in preheated oven for about 10 minutes. Do not allow the sugar to melt. Remove baking sheet to cooling rack while preparing the custard. Increase oven temperature to 325 degrees. Lightly butter bottom and sides of six (6-ounce) ramekins; set aside.

Combine the whipping cream, sugar, chocolate, and cocoa in a heavy 2-quart saucepan over medium heat. Whisking often, cook until chocolate is melted and sugar has dissolved. Remove from heat and set aside to cool.

Combine the egg yolks, vanilla extract, and softened goat cheese in work bowl of food processor fitted with steel blade. Process until smooth and well blended. Turn the egg mixture out into a medium bowl and whisk in the chocolate mixture until smooth. Divide the mixture among the prepared ramekins and place the ramekins in a baking dish. Add enough hot water to reach halfway up the sides of the ramekins. Bake in preheated oven for 1 hour. Remove ramekins from baking dish and refrigerate until the custard is thoroughly chilled, at least 6 hours.

Put the cooled brown sugar in work bowl of food processor fitted with steel blade or an electric coffee grinder and process until the sugar is very fine. Set aside.

When the custard is well chilled, place the ramekins on a baking sheet and divide the brown sugar among the ramekins, spreading a thin layer on top of each one. Using a culinary blowtorch, caramelize the sugar, taking care not to burn it. (Or if you don't own such a gadget, preheat the broiler and place the oven rack 3 inches under the heat source. Place the baking sheet under the broiler and cook just until the sugar has caramelized.) Allow the sugar to harden for a few minutes, and then serve.

(Terry Thompson-Anderson)

Bradley Goat Farms

Lampasas

Lou Bradley is an authentic Texas treasure. A fourth-generation Texan, she and her husband moved to the Hill Country after Dave's retirement from the air force ended their prolonged odyssey of travel. The Bradleys have been in Lampasas for thirty-one years now, and Lou's been making goat cheese for twenty-five of those years. ❖ Soon after they had purchased the fifteen acres adjacent to their original seven-acre property, the Lampasas school district decided to raise taxes—a lot. Several hundred protestors attended the next school board meeting, and right in the middle of a rowdy group on the front row was Lou Bradley. Finally, one of the school board members leaned over to her and said, "Lou, get goats, declare the land for agriculture, sit down, and shut up!" She went home and told her husband that they were getting some goats. She had no earthly idea what she would do with goats, but she wasn't about to pay those taxes! Not long ago Dave observed that maybe they should have paid those taxes instead of working so hard in their "retirement." ❖ What to do with a herd of Nubian and Alpine goats? Lou decided to open a goat's milk dairy and taught herself how to make cheese by reading

and experimenting. Her first milk inspector encouraged her to get a license to manufacture cheese after tasting some of her trial batches. Boy, did she get it right—her goat cheese is some of the best I've ever had. But it isn't available in stores. You can buy Bradley Goat Farms cheeses only at the farm. Give Lou a call to be sure she has a good supply, and tell her when you'd like to come. ❖ Lou makes two types of cheese: soft chèvre and semi-hard. The mind literally races with the possible uses for her four flavors of soft chèvre: Plain, Green Chile, Chipotle, and Sun-Dried Tomato & Garlic! And her semi-hard cheese has a delicate earthy taste and a firm, almost crumbly texture; soaked in Cabernet Sauvignon, it's the perfect foil for the deep berry nuances of the wine. Don't need to think about a use for that one—just get out the cheese knife! Make the trip to Lampasas, and be sure to take along a big cooler.

1046 BCR 111 • (512) 556-3109

Eve's Café

Lampasas

Eve's Café is located in a charming building right on the square in downtown Lampasas, a picturesque Hill Country town in which life goes on much the way it always has—at a slower pace than the rest of the world. But there's nothing slow about the pace in the kitchen at Eve's. On Friday nights the place is standing-room-only. ❧ Eve Sanchez was born and raised in the small German town of Fulda, just north of Frankfurt. She married an American GI stationed in Germany, and her

husband's eventual transfer to Fort Hood in Killeen brought Eve to the United States and its myriad opportunities. ❧ She began to muse on the fact that she had spent her whole life working for other people—and working very hard. So why not take that same capacity for hard work and put it to use in a place of her own? When her husband retired, the Sanchezes moved to Lampasas, where Eve discovered the wealth of German heritage in the surrounding small towns of the Hill Country. ❧ In 1995 Eve and her husband, Steve, opened Eve's Café, which quickly became a favorite dining spot in Lampasas, serving breakfast and lunch from Monday through Thursday and also dinner on

Fridays. The Sanchezes' son, Marc, has stepped in to run the place, but you'll still see Eve there most of the time when the restaurant is open. ❧ At Eve's you won't find sausage plates drowned in limp red cabbage or bland sauerkraut with a side of watery potatoes. What you will find is food from the small German villages, prepared in the traditional manner. Eve's specialty is pork schnitzel. In fact, Eve's serves just the kind of food that probably sustained the early German pioneers in the area. Eve's is a special treat right in the heart of the Texas Hill Country!

521 E. 3rd Street • (512) 556-3500

HOUSE SALAD

When sharing this recipe, Eve said, "You must have the German white vinegar! It won't work with other kinds of vinegar." And, of course, she was right. I tried it with several kinds of vinegar readily available at the supermarket, and it truly wasn't the same. So head for the specialty markets and scout out authentic imported German vinegar. Prepare the dressing at least 2 hours before serving and chill it well.

Yield: 6 servings

1 head romaine lettuce, cut into slices 1½ inches
   thick
Sliced cucumber
Thin-sliced red onion

House Dressing

2 green onions, minced
3 fresh dill sprigs, minced
1½ cups whipping cream
½ cup whole milk
3 tablespoons German white vinegar
1 tablespoon sugar
1 teaspoon salt

Make the House Dressing. Combine the green onions and dill in a medium bowl. Whisk in the cream and milk, blending well, then slowly whisk in the vinegar to form a smooth mixture. Whisk in the sugar and salt. If the dressing is too thick, add additional milk, a little at a time, whisking to blend. Adjust seasoning as needed. Cover and refrigerate until well chilled, or at least 2 hours.

To assemble the salad, place a portion of the romaine on each salad plate and drizzle a portion of dressing over the top. Arrange 3 or 4 cucumber slices on each salad and scatter a few of the thin-sliced red onions on top.

(Eve's Café)

BUTTERMILK PIE

The recipe for this sinfully delicious pie was given to Bonnie over thirty years ago by a "precious little old ranch woman." The crust is one you'll want to use often. Bonnie says you just can't have a good pie without a good crust.

Yield: Two 9-inch pies

Crust

1¾ cups all-purpose flour

1¼ sticks margarine at room temperature

1 egg, beaten

1 teaspoon vinegar

2 tablespoons ice-cold water

Filling

3½ cups sugar

2 tablespoons all-purpose flour

6 eggs, beaten

1 cup buttermilk

2 teaspoons vanilla extract

¼ pound (1 stick) margarine, melted

Make the crust. Blend the flour and margarine in a large bowl using a pastry blender until the mixture resembles coarse grain. Add the egg, vinegar, and cold water. Mix well, but don't overmix. Divide the dough into two equal portions and roll out on a floured work surface. Chill while preparing the filling. (Chilling prevents shrinking.)

Preheat oven to 300 degrees. To make the filling, combine the sugar and flour in a large bowl, tossing with a fork to blend. Add the beaten eggs, buttermilk, vanilla, and melted margarine. Stir mixture just until well blended; don't beat it. Pour into the chilled pie crust and bake in preheated oven for about 1½ hours, or until the filling doesn't jiggle in the middle when you shake it. Chill before slicing.

(Bonnie's Bakery)

Bonnie's Bakery

Leakey

Bonnie Crider, a dynamo of a lady, moved from Houston in 1970 to the Frio Canyon, where her husband's family owned Crider's Cabins, a resort on the Frio River just south of Leakey. Bonnie opened her first restaurant, Country Kitchen, and became known for her delicious foods, especially her pies and other baked goods. ❀ In 1987 Bonnie took over management of Crider's Cabins and decided to give up the restaurant business, focusing on her first love in the kitchen: baking.

Thus began Bonnie's Bakery. In the early days she'd put a couple of pies in the oven, then run and clean a cabin. Over the years both businesses grew, and now she has three employees in the bakery, but she still manages the cabins. ❀ Folks start lining up outside the door of the tiny bakery before 7:30 in the morning. Bonnie will have the coffee on and plenty of hot doughnuts and her incredible cinnamon rolls, along with a display case full of other goodies. Stacked around the bakery you'll see parts of wedding cakes she'll deliver in the afternoon and various other special-order cakes, pies, cookies, and pastries. Bonnie will also ship her tempting treats (see the Web site for details).

❀ She said the best compliment she ever received was from a man who visited the bakery often. He said, "Bonnie, I don't know if you're making any money here, but you sure are making a lot of folks happy."

U.S. 83 (between RR 1120 and RR 1050) • (830) 232-5584 • www.cridersonthe-frio.com/bakery.htm

CHICKEN AND SAUSAGE GUMBO

You can vary the taste of this delicious gumbo by using duck meat as a substitute for the chicken.

Yield: 8 to 10 servings

3 cups Gumbo Roux (see recipe below)

2 medium onions, chopped

2 large green bell peppers, chopped

3 large celery stalks, chopped

2 tablespoons minced flat-leaf parsley

2 teaspoons minced fresh thyme

½ teaspoon freshly ground black pepper

3 fresh bay leaves, minced

1 teaspoon minced fresh marjoram

2 heaping tablespoons filé powder

1 pound CrawLinks sausage links

2 quarts homemade duck or chicken stock

1 cup dry vermouth

2 pounds cooked chicken meat, cut into bite-size pieces, or substitute duck meat

1 teaspoon red (cayenne) pepper, or to taste

Salt to taste

Cooked white rice

Sliced green onions for garnish

Gumbo Roux

3 cups solid vegetable shortening or lard

3 cups all-purpose flour

Preheat oven to 350 degrees. Make the Gumbo Roux. Heat shortening in a heavy, deep-sided 12-inch skillet over medium heat. When the fat is hot, add the flour all at once and whisk until well blended and smooth. Continue to cook, whisking constantly, until roux is a deep mahogany color, about 30 minutes.

Add the vegetables and all seasonings except cayenne and salt. Cook the vegetables, stirring often, until they are very wilted and the onions are translucent, about 15 minutes. Remove from heat and set aside. While the vegetables are cooking, arrange the sausage links on a baking sheet and bake in preheated oven for about 10 minutes, or until the fat has been rendered. Pat the sausage links with paper towels to remove all traces of fat, then slice into bite-size pieces and set aside.

Bring the stock to a full boil in a 10-quart soup pot. Add the roux and vegetable mixture to the boiling stock; boil vigorously for 10 minutes, stirring frequently. Stir in the vermouth, chicken, and cooked sausage and boil for an additional 10 minutes. Lower heat and season with cayenne and salt. Cover and simmer for 45 minutes.

To serve, spoon about ⅔ cup cooked white rice into each serving bowl; ladle the gumbo over the rice. Garnish with green onions. Serve hot.

(Terry Thompson-Anderson)

Texas Cajun Sausage Company

Leakey

John L. Price is a really likeable guy who owns a ranch outside of Leakey. He considers himself primarily a rancher, but back in the spring of 2003, he began playing around with recipes for sausage. Eventually he came up with a sausage made from crawfish tails and pork. Everybody loved it, so John formed the Texas Cajun Sausage Company to sell and distribute the sausage under the trade name CrawLinks. Then he found a USDA-inspected facility to produce it in commercial quantities according to his recipe. ❀ Chances are, if you attend many festivals in Texas, you'll run into John and his CrawLinks. You can also order fully cooked, frozen CrawLinks from the Web site. The site also provides a list of the festivals where you can taste and purchase the sausage. John plans to add more retail outlets for the sausage in the future. ❀ CrawLinks is a really bodacious sausage. It's good and spicy and has just the right ratio of meat to fat. It's perfect in gumbo, on a sausage po'boy, or just to grill and eat.

1520 Old Reagan Wells Road • (830) 232-4424 • www.gocajun.com

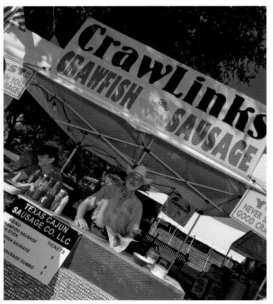

Berry Street Bakery

Llano

When Christine and Frank DeLapp opened Berry Street Bakery in 2004 in a charming old house across from the courthouse, it quickly became a gathering spot for locals, and some admit to eating here several times a week. The bakery is known for its delicious breads, pastries, cakes, and cookies and as a great place for breakfast and lunch. ❦ But in 2011, when the DeLapps wanted to retire, their long-time friend and coworker at the bakery, Joanna Russell, simply would not accept this decision. Joanna loved the

bakery as much as the DeLapps did and asked them if they would consider selling it to her. It was a prayer answered for the DeLapps, as they hated the thought of simply closing what had become a local institution. ❦ Joanna comes from a very self-reliant family. Her dad raised livestock for their table, and there was always a big vegetable garden. She grew up watching her grandmother and mother bake and learned basic cooking skills from both. But she credits Christine with honing those skills to a professional level. She loves custom-baking cakes for special occasions as much as her customers love the finished products. ❦ In January of 2012 Joanna took over the bakery and, with Christine's help, made a few structural changes to the interior, which allowed her to increase the seating. She added some additional breakfast items and expanded the lunch menu with additional salads and sandwiches as well as a hot meal that changes weekly along with the soup. She's

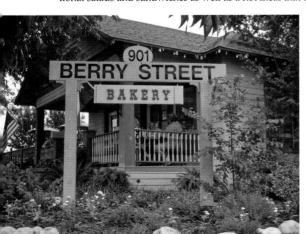

kept the same cozy feel in the dining areas, with the quaint collection of old salt and pepper shakers still residing on the tables. And the coffee's always on—hot and fresh. She wants to add cheese plates to the menu with a selection of Texas artisan cheeses and fruits to go with the bakery's great breads, which Frank DeLapp still bakes for her.

901 Berry Street • (325) 247-1855 • www.berrystreetbakery.com

HOUSE GRANOLA

Berry Street Bakery sells this delicious granola in small bags displayed on top of the bakery counter. It's easy to make and would make great hostess gifts or Christmas gifts, sealed in zip-sealing bags and packed inside colorful tins.

Yield: About 1 gallon

1 cup dried cranberries
1 cup dark raisins
1 cup golden raisins
1 cup mixed dried fruit
¾ cup canola oil
1½ cups honey
1 teaspoon cinnamon
4 cups rolled oats
4 cups wheat flakes
2 cups sunflower seeds
2 cups raw wheat germ
1 cup chopped pecans
1 cup sliced unskinned almonds
1 cup whole almonds
1½ cups coconut

Preheat oven to 325 degrees. Combine the fruits in a bowl and toss to blend; set aside. Combine the canola oil, honey, and cinnamon in a bowl, whisking until well blended; set aside. In a large bowl combine all remaining ingredients. Pour the oil mixture over the dry ingredients in the large bowl. Stir to mix well. Spread the mixture out in a thin layer on baking sheets. Toast in preheated oven for 10 to 15 minutes, or until light golden brown. Do not overcook. Remove from oven and cool on wire racks. When completely cool, turn the mixture out into a large bowl and mix in the reserved fruits. Store in an airtight container.

(Berry Street Bakery)

U. S. POST-OFFICE
1850 LUCKENBACH, TX. 1971

LUCKENBACH

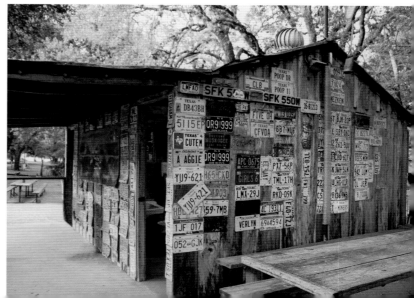

Luckenbach Feed Lot

Luckenbach

Luckenbach, located off Ranch Road 1376 about thirteen miles southeast of Fredericksburg, is a tiny, scenic community that has gained cult status. It all began in the early 1970s when rancher and folklorist Russell (Hondo) Crouch bought the entire town, proclaimed himself mayor, and turned the old store/saloon and dance hall into a showcase for Texas "outlaw" country music. He also coined the phrase that now adorns t-shirts around the world: "Everybody's Somebody in Luckenbach." After Jerry Jeff Walker and his band recorded the album ¡Viva Terlingua! live at the Luckenbach Dance Hall, thousands of music fans began to descend on the town. Four years later, it was memorialized by Waylon Jennings and Wil-

lie Nelson with their song "Luckenbach, Texas." ❈ No visit to Luckenbach is complete without tasting the made-from-scratch cowboy grub at the Luckenbach Feed Lot. Its exceptional pulled pork sandwich, made

famous by the late Richard Tanner, is still served by his wife, Socorro. She also offers up lots of munchies to enjoy with the cold beer from the saloon, including hand-breaded fried dill pickle slices and jalapeño poppers, along with great burgers and sausage in many forms—sandwiches, wraps, and on a stick. Socorro hand-cuts the potatoes for her legendary curly fries and then cooks them to order. Her Frito pie is a delicious version of this iconic Texas dish. Have a hankering for something sweet? Try Socorro's old-fashioned funnel cakes or an order of crisp, airy sopapillas, or even fried cheesecake!

412 Luckenbach Town Loop • (830) 997-3224

PHOTOGRAPHS BY ROBBYN DODD

COCONUT MERINGUE PIE

Yield: One 9-inch pie

One baked 9-inch pie crust

Filling

1 cup sugar
¼ cup cornstarch
¼ teaspoon salt
3 cups whole milk
4 egg yolks (reserve whites)
3 tablespoons butter
1½ teaspoons vanilla extract
1 (3½-ounce) can sweetened flaked coconut

Meringue

4 egg whites at room temperature
¼ teaspoon cream of tartar
½ cup sugar
½ teaspoon vanilla extract
Toasted coconut

To make the filling, combine the sugar, cornstarch, salt, and milk in a heavy 3-quart saucepan over medium heat. Cook, stirring constantly until the mixture boils and thickens, then cook for an additional 2 minutes. Remove from heat and set aside. In a separate bowl, beat the egg yolks. Whisking vigorously, slowly stir 1 cup of the hot milk mixture into the yolks. Stir the warmed yolks into the remainder of the milk mixture and bring to a gentle boil. Cook, stirring, for 2 minutes. Remove from heat and add the butter and vanilla, stirring until the butter has melted. Add the coconut, blending well. Pour into the baked pie crust and set aside.

Preheat oven to 350 degrees. Make the meringue. Using an electric mixer, beat the egg whites and cream of tartar at high speed until foamy. Gradually add the sugar, 1 tablespoon at a time, until stiff peaks form and the sugar is dissolved, about 2 to 4 minutes. Add vanilla and beat just to blend. Spread the meringue over the hot filling, sealing it to the edge of the pastry. Sprinkle with toasted coconut. Bake in preheated oven for 12 to 15 minutes, or until lightly browned. Cool completely before slicing.

(Blue Bonnet Café)

Blue Bonnet Café

Marble Falls

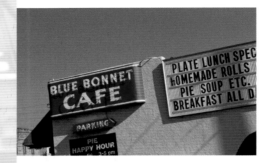

The Blue Bonnet Café is an institution, having been a fact of daily life in Marble Falls since 1929. It's one of those places where the locals gather and everybody seems to know the person at the next table. ❈ Originally located on Main Street, the café moved to its present site "on the highway" in 1946. It quickly became a favorite stopping place for folks who were just passing through town. Today you just might see a famous country western singer, movie star, NFL great, or other celebrity bellied up to the counter or settled into a booth, chowing down on the famous grub for which the café has always been known. The café has been written up in hundreds of publications from coast to coast. ❈ John and Belinda Kemper bought the Blue Bonnet in 1981 and set about to not change a thing! They had been in the hospitality and food business for most of their lives and were thrilled to own such a legend. ❈ When the Kempers' daughter, Lindsay, was an exchange student in high school, she took some Blue Bonnet Café t-shirts to her host family in Australia. The father was working on a project in Antarctica and one day wore his t-shirt to work. Another man pointed to the shirt and said, "The Blue Bonnet? I'm from Spicewood, Texas, and I eat there all the time when I'm home." ❈ The staff is very much like a big, happy extended family. The waitresses are some of the friendliest you'll find anywhere—despite the fact that on an average day the Blue Bonnet serves 2,000 meals! And they're open seven days a week. Breakfast is served all day, and a daily hot lunch special is served from 11 a.m. until closing time. Dinner is served every day except Sunday. It's true comfort food, complete with plate-size chicken-fried steak with cream gravy and mashed potatoes. Big, puffy yeast rolls are served with hot meals, and they'll keep bringing them as often as you ask! ❈ But the real draw at the Blue Bonnet is the impressive array of homemade pies of every description, displayed in the pie case at the entrance to the dining room. You can buy a slice or the whole pie. They're as good as they look, too. The Coconut Meringue is by far the most popular. ❈ Lindsay and her husband, David, are taking over the reins at the café, giving Mom and Dad a little breather. But you'll still find John there most mornings, shaking hands with regulars and greeting the first-timers.

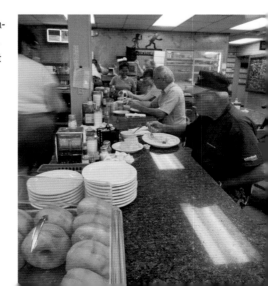

211 U.S. 281 • (830) 693-2444 •
www.highlandlakes.com/bluebonnet

Brothers Bakery & Café

Marble Falls

Brothers Bakery & Café, which opened in 2002, was the culmination of a lifetime dream. Chef Ryan LeCompte Malamud, the owner, was born in New Orleans to a family whose life revolved around great food. The family moved to Georgetown, Texas, when Ryan was six. As a high school senior, Ryan was one of the first students to enroll in a newly offered culinary class, fueling his growing interest in pursuing a career in food. After graduation he traveled extensively in Europe, working in bakeries in Italy, France, Spain, and the Netherlands, learning the techniques of fine European baking as well as bakery operations. After returning to the United States he earned a degree from the Culinary Institute of America in Hyde Park, New York, and then went on to pursue a degree in baking and pastry arts from the Institute's Napa Valley campus in 2001. ❦ Ryan named the bakery in honor of his brother Kurt, who lives in Louisiana but works with Ryan at the bakery several times a year when he comes to visit. ❦ The bakery makes pastries, muffins, breads, cookies, pies, quiches, and the most incredible French-style croissants you'll find in the Hill Country. Ryan worked painstakingly on the recipe to achieve a perfect European-style pastry. He uses real butter in all of the pastries, never manufactured, "fake" fats. The cakes are not only luscious but beautiful creations made with real buttercream icing. The bakery serves lunch each day—soups, sandwiches, and innovative salads, all made from scratch.

The sandwiches, naturally, are served on house-made artisan breads. It's a busy place with lots of hustle and bustle in the open kitchen behind the pastry case. There are racks of fresh breads of every description. The pastry case itself is about 8 feet of temptation, crammed with mouth-watering goodies. ❦ You'll run into Ryan at restaurants and resorts all over the Hill Country as he makes deliveries for his thriving wholesale business, which provides baked goods to fine dining establishments.

519 U.S. 281 North (at 6th Street) •
(830) 798-8278 • www.brothersbakery.com

AMY'S FAVORITE COOKIES

Ryan named these really great cookies after his cousin Amy, who thinks they're great, too.

1 cup butter
2 cups sugar
3 eggs
½ teaspoon allspice
1 teaspoon ground cinnamon
1 teaspoon baking soda
1 teaspoon vanilla extract
2 teaspoons salt
1 teaspoon baking powder
2 cups chopped pecans
5 cups all-purpose flour

Preheat oven to 350 degrees. In bowl of electric mixer, cream the butter and sugar together until fluffy and light in color, 4 to 5 minutes. Add the eggs, one at a time, scraping down the sides of the bowl after each addition. Add spices, baking soda, vanilla, and salt, beating just to blend. In a separate bowl combine the baking powder, pecans, and flour, whisking to blend well. Add the flour mixture to the butter mixture and blend well, scraping down the sides of the bowl often. Drop the batter by teaspoonfuls onto a cookie sheet. Bake in preheated oven for 10 to 12 minutes. Cool on a wire rack.

(Ryan LeCompte Malamud)

Flat Creek Estate
Marble Falls

Rick and Madelyn Naber jokingly say that they purchased this eighty-acre property, formerly a Limousin cattle ranch, because of its attributes, not because the location was convenient to anywhere! ❀ Wanting to maintain the land's agricultural character, the Nabers made exhaustive soil and water tests, all of which confirmed that the site—with its deep soils, natural springs, and sloping hillsides—was ideal for viticulture. Vines were first planted on six acres in 2000, and this has now expanded to twenty acres of vineyards. A 5,000-case winery was constructed in 2001. Along with such signature varietals as sangiovese, shiraz, and Portuguese port varietals, Flat Creek Estate produces noteworthy wines from muscat, tempranillo, and pinot grigio grapes. ❀ Flat Creek's winemaker, Tim Drake, hails from Washington State, where he worked at Columbia Crest Winery and Chateau Ste. Michelle. In 2005, he went to work as cellar master at Matthews Cellars, a Washington State producer of high-end wines. In 2009 Tim and his family decided that, after thirty-nine years of the Seattle climate, they were ready for a change and headed for Texas, where Tim was eager to get involved with the growing wine industry here. He met Rick Naber at a meeting of the Texas Wine and Grape Growers Association and took over as winemaker at Flat Creek in 2011. ❀ The Nabers are committed to producing quality Texas wines under two labels. The Flat Creek Estate label is devoted to estate-grown fruit and includes Pinot Grigio, Muscato Blanco, Shiraz, and "Super Texan" Sangiovese wines. The Travis Peak Select label presents a broader range of wines, crafted entirely from Texas fruit, including Cabernet Sauvignon and Orange Muscat. Flat Creek wines have won many awards and accolades. A grand facility with an event center and tasting room offers a spectacular view of the vineyards and a perfect venue for wine releases, cooking classes, weddings, banquets, and other events.

24912 Singleton Bend East Road (off FM 1431) • (512) 267-6310 • www.flatcreekestate.com

Noon Spoon Café
Marble Falls

Jennifer Cayce doesn't call herself a chef. She refers to the food she serves at the Noon Spoon Café as "upscale comfort food." It's a style of cooking she learned when she was quite young. "I had my own little stool that I would pull up to the kitchen counter at my grandmother's, or in my mother's kitchen, and harass them both to teach me how to cook," Jennifer recalls. ❁ She went on to complete a degree in nutritional science, and

in 1998 she opened a delivery-only diner that she later sold. In 2008 she opened the Noon Spoon Café in an attractive building with a bright blue tin roof. The open spaces of the café are well utilized and very pleasant, with simple furnishings, vivid but attractive color combinations, and natural wood architectural features. ❁ The café is open for breakfast and lunch from Monday through Friday, with breakfast served all day. The menu offers a number of tempting breakfast items, a stunning array of soups, salads, sandwiches, and wraps, and a unique chili pie, Daily Special plate lunches, and made-from-scratch home-style desserts. Many items can be ordered in large quantities to go. Jennifer is a self-confessed food snob, which she says makes her very particular in the selection of the ingredients she uses. She's a stickler for freshness, making food in small batches each day.

Her goal is to offer the healthiest food possible without compromising the flavor and excitement of a dish. She loves what she's doing, and that attitude has helped make the café a well-loved and successful venture.

610 Broadway Street • (830) 798-2347 • www.noonspooncafe.com

JENNIFER CAYCE'S CHEESY SPINACH BREAD

Jennifer loves this recipe, but it's her brother John who thinks it's the greatest bread on the planet. He calls her every time he makes it to be sure he's not leaving anything out!

Yield: 8 to 10 servings

- 1 loaf of crusty French bread, cut in half lengthwise using a serrated knife
- 2 tablespoons butter
- 4 garlic cloves, minced
- ½ of a white onion, cut into ¼-inch dice
- 1 large portabella mushroom, cleaned and cut into bite-size cubes
- 2 pounds baby spinach
- 6 ounces shredded Chihuahua cheese, or substitute Monterey Jack cheese
- 3 tablespoons whipping cream
- Salt and pepper to taste
- Diced, garden-fresh tomatoes

Preheat oven to 400 degrees. Line a baking sheet with parchment paper; place the halves of the French bread, cut sides up, on the baking sheet; set aside. Melt the butter in a deep-sided skillet over medium heat. Add the garlic and onion and sauté for 5 minutes. Add the mushroom cubes and cook for 5 minutes. Add the spinach and cook until wilted. Add the cheese and cream. Cook over low heat, stirring constantly, until cheese has melted. Season with salt and pepper. Divide the spinach mixture equally and spread evenly on the two bread halves. Bake in preheated oven until the topping is lightly browned and bubbly, about 8 minutes. Remove from oven and scatter the tomatoes over the loaves. Allow to cool for a few minutes, then slice into 1½-inch slices using a serrated knife; serve.

(Jennifer Cayce)

BLACKBERRY CROSTADA WITH STREUSEL TOPPING

A crostada is a free-form pastry that can be filled with many kinds of fruit and berries. They are really quick and easy to make. Don't worry about the final shape of the crostada—the rustic look is part of its homemade charm. It's an all-around winner when made with fresh-from-the-vine Texas blackberries.

Yield: 6 to 8 servings

Chilled whipping cream

Pastry

1 cup all-purpose flour

Pinch of salt

¼ pound (1 stick) frozen unsalted butter, cut into 1-inch cubes

3 to 4 tablespoons very cold water

Filling

1 pint (2 heaping cups) fresh blackberries

1 teaspoon finely minced lemon zest

⅔ cup sugar

½ cup raspberry liqueur

Streusel Topping

3 tablespoons unsalted butter, cut into small cubes

1 teaspoon vanilla

½ cup all-purpose flour

½ cup sugar

To make the pastry, combine the flour, salt, and butter in work bowl of food processor fitted with steel blade. Pulse until the butter is broken up into pea-size bits. Add 3 tablespoons of the cold water and process until well blended. Check the consistency of the dough by gathering a small amount into your hand and squeezing. It should form a ball.

(continued)

Sweet Berry Farm

Marble Falls

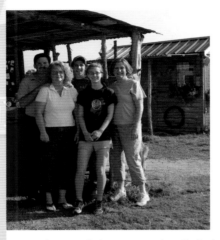

Sweet Berry Farm is a family destination on Saturdays and Sundays. It's exactly what Dan and Gretchen Copeland envisioned when they started the twenty-acre "pick-your-own" farm outside Marble Falls in 1999. ❀ Here you can pick as many strawberries, blackberries, tomatoes, potatoes, pumpkins, and gourds in their respective seasons as you can haul away. The Copelands will even provide clippers and gloves for those thorny blackberry vines. Except for the pumpkins and gourds (which are priced individually), you pay for fruit by the pound. ❀ But be sure to pack a lunch. After Mom, Dad, and the kids have picked for a while, everybody can ramble down to the covered arbor and have a bona fide picnic. Don't worry about bringing dessert, though—the farm sells homemade ice cream, made with the farm's own fruit, as well as awesome smoothies and shakes. The homemade strawberry preserves are also mighty fine. ❀ You'll probably be met by Dan's father, Max Copeland, who is the official greeter at Sweet Berry Farm. He retired after forty years of being a pastor in Marble Falls. Max will certainly steer you to the Texas Maze, an immensely popular feature at the farm. It's a four-acre maze formed by eight-foot-high sorghum-sudan grass cut in the shape of Texas. Within the maze are numerous paths and almost a dozen "cities" at points that approximate their real geographical locations in Texas. There's a new game theme each spring and summer. You get cards revealing the theme and you have to find the cities—and then find your way out! Also for the kids there are goats, donkeys, and horses for petting.

**1801 FM 1980 •
(830) 798-1462 •
www.sweetberry-farm.com**

If the dough is too dry to form a ball, add the remaining 1 tablespoon water, or more if needed. Process just until water is blended. (Don't allow the dough to form a ball in the processor.) Turn crumbly dough out onto a work surface and knead together three or four times to form a cohesive dough. There should still be chunks of butter in the dough. Pat dough into a disk, wrap in plastic wrap, and refrigerate for 20 minutes.

Preheat oven to 375 degrees. Line a 14-inch-wide baking sheet with parchment paper; set aside.

To make the filling, combine all ingredients in a medium bowl and stir to blend, taking care not to break up the berries. Set aside.

Make the Streusel Topping. Combine all ingredients in work bowl of food processor fitted with steel blade and pulse until the mixture is crumbly; set aside.

To assemble the crostada, turn the pastry out onto a floured work surface and roll into a 12-inch round. Roll the pastry around the rolling pin and unroll it onto the parchment-lined baking sheet. Using a slotted spoon, spoon the berry filling into the center of the pastry. Discard the juice from the bowl. Working quickly, fold the edge of the dough up around the berries in a pleated fashion, leaving about 4 to 5 inches of exposed berries in the center. Scatter the Streusel Topping over the entire crostada; bake in preheated oven for 30 to 35 minutes, or until the pastry is golden brown and the filling is bubbly and has formed a nice syrup. Slide the crostada onto a wire rack by lifting both sides of the parchment paper. Cool until lukewarm, then slice into wedges. Serve in shallow bowls, drizzling whipping cream over each serving.

(Terry Thompson-Anderson)

Akashic Vineyard
Mason

"**S**nip at the top of the grape cluster—and no MOG" (material other than grapes), intoned Akashic Vineyard owner Don Pullum as the group of volunteer grape pickers headed to the 1.5-acre section of the vineyard planted in mourvèdre grapes, buckets and clippers in hand. ❄ Each year at harvest time volunteers show up from all over the Hill Country and from all walks of

life to help with the harvest. They go down the rows singing songs and telling tales while filling five-gallon buckets with grapes. When all the fruit has been picked, it will be hauled to Sandstone Cellars Winery in Mason, where Don is also the winemaker. After being crushed, the grapes will go into the fermentation tanks where the process of making another vintage of fine wine will begin. ❄ How did an Ivy League–educated venture capitalist, with no family ties to agriculture, come to be the steward of seven and a half acres of grapevines? Don says that he began his lifelong love of wine at age sixteen when he was given a small pour of a Chablis Premier Cru from the estate of Albert Pic. He knew the wine was good but lacked the sensory recall and vocabulary to describe its bouquet. It simply tasted good. ❄ While working in Houston, Don met the late Camille Berman, the wickedly charismatic owner of Maxim's Restaurant. Camille liked Don and became his friend and wine mentor. ❄ In 1998 Don found the land for his vineyard and planted the first vines, an acre of primitivo grapes, followed in subsequent years by plantings of grenache, sangiovese, mourvèdre, and syrah. ❄ The first commercial wine that Don crafted was the 2004 Sandstone Cellars Syrah, released in November of 2005. It was a very good vintage. As the vines mature, the vineyard continues to produce excellent fruit each year. ❄ Akashic Vineyard is not open to the public, but serious oenophiles may call to arrange a tour or to volunteer for picking.

Bluff Creek Road • (325) 265-4221

Sandstone Cellars Winery

Mason

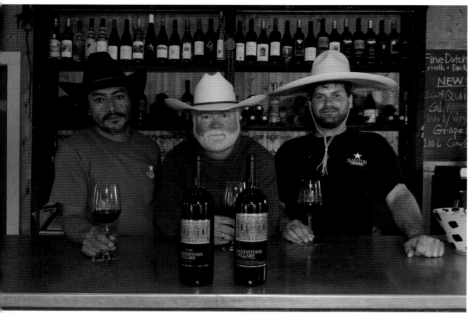

Sandstone Cellars is a small boutique winery in one of the Hill Country's newest wine regions, Mason County, which is proving to be excellent for growing grapes. The Hickory Sands soil and moderate weather seem to be a particularly good match for growing Mediterranean grape varietals. ❋ Sandstone Cellars, the first winery to open in Mason County, was established by partners Manny Silerio and Scott Haupert in 2003 after state laws were passed allowing wineries to operate tasting rooms in dry counties. The winery is located in a charming raised cottage across from the courthouse on Mason's town square. ❋ Scott and Manny met while both were in college in San Antonio—Manny a business major and Scott a journalism major. Scott's real love, however, was the viola. Classically trained, Scott went on to receive a master's degree in music performance from Yale. The pair moved to Los Angeles, where Manny became a merchandiser for Gap clothing stores while Scott pursued a professional music career, playing on more than 300 film scores, including *Fried Green Tomatoes, Jurassic Park,* and *All the Pretty Horses.*

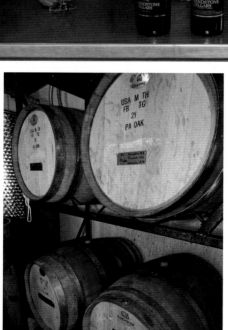

Scott appeared twice on *The Tonight Show* with Jay Leno and has performed on over 100 recordings, including orchestral backup for Barbra Streisand. ❋ The winemaker at Sandstone Cellars is Don Pullum, who was the first to plant wine grapes in Mason County, starting with one acre of grapes on his Akashic Vineyard property in 1998. ❋ Sandstone Cellars released its first wine, a Syrah, in 2005, followed in 2006 by Sandstone II, a blend of eight Mediterranean varietals. Both wines have met with critical acclaim. Sandstone II was awarded a bronze medal at the 2007 San Francisco Wine Fair Competition, one of the country's most prestigious wine competitions, beating out some very respected California vintners for the title. Sandstone III, released in 2007, was another great vintage. ❋ With a track record of three out of three wines being far superior to the norm, it's a safe bet that we'll hear more great things about these guys. ❋ The winery is also a good place to purchase noteworthy wines from other Texas wineries, some of which do not have tasting rooms.

211 San Antonio Street (U.S. 87) • (325) 347-9463 • www.sandstonecellarswinery.com

Santos Taqueria y Cantina

Mason

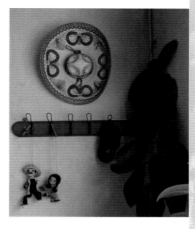

During the lunch or dinner hour from Thursday through Saturday and at lunchtime on Sundays, there's standing room only at Santos Taqueria. This small taqueria and cantina—owned by Sandstone Cellars Winery partners Manny Silerio and Scott Haupert, along with Manny's mom, Santos—is a favorite with locals. Santos Taqueria y Cantina has been named as one of the Hill Country's 25 Best Places by *Texas Monthly* and praised in many other publications. ❧ Located on the town square in a refurbished gas station, the taqueria is a unique place. There are a few tables and a couple of booths inside, plus a spacious covered patio outside where the gas pumps used to be. The grounds have been lushly landscaped, so it's enjoyable to sit outside and watch the goings-on in Mason. ❧ Santos Silerio not only runs the kitchen but also prepares most of the food herself. And it's all made from scratch, just the way her grandmother taught her. ❧ You'll find such sinfully delicious gems as gorditas with your choice of fillings. Gorditas are a deep-fried pocket made from corn masa and stuffed with various ingredients. They're hard to find at Mexican restaurants because they're so time-consuming to make—and they're only as good as the filling! ❧ The menu also features chalupas, taquitos, quesadillas, nachos, and a fabulous Chile con Queso. Whatever your preference, it's all great. ❧ Santos Taqueria makes four different salsas fresh each day, all distinctively and deliciously different from any other salsas. ❧ Scott and Manny often do double duty at both the winery and the taqueria, working behind the counter or cleaning tables. And Santos will be scurrying around in the open kitchen, patting out gorditas or tending

orders on the stove. ❧ You can purchase a bottle of wine at the winery and take it next door to the taqueria to enjoy with your lunch. Any one of the three Sandstone vintages would be perfect with an item from the taqueria menu. ❧ It's a busy little place, and that's part of its charm, coupled with the fact that Scott, Manny, and Santos are just good folks.

205 San Antonio Street (U.S. 87) • (325) 347-6140

NOPALES Y PUERCO DURANGO STYLE

This delicious pork dish is often served in Mexican homes. You won't find it on the menu at Santos Taqueria, but Santos was kind enough to contribute the recipe for this book. If fresh nopales (nopal cactus pads) aren't available, you can substitute canned nopales. Santos recommends the Dona Maria brand.

Yield: 6 to 8 servings

5 to 7 fresh nopales, cut into ½-inch dice (7 cups)
13 cups water
3 teaspoons salt
Half of an onion, peeled
1 cup chopped cilantro
4 garlic cloves
10 dried New Mexico or cascabel chilies, stems and seeds removed
3 tablespoons canola oil
4 pounds pork butt, cut into ¾-inch cubes
2 teaspoons masa
⅛ teaspoon ground cumin
1 teaspoon dried Mexican oregano, crushed
¼ teaspoon red (cayenne) pepper, if desired, or more to taste

In a heavy Dutch oven over medium-high heat, combine the nopales, 5 cups of the water, 1½ teaspoons of the salt, onion, cilantro, and 2 of the garlic cloves. Bring to a boil, lower heat to medium, and cook, uncovered, for 20 minutes. Drain the nopales in a colander and set aside. Discard cooking water.

Place the dried chilies in a heavy 3-quart saucepan. Add just enough water to cover and bring to a full boil, then turn off the heat and let cool slightly. Transfer the chilies and cooking water to a blender; add the remaining 2 garlic cloves and puree until smooth.

Heat the canola oil in the Dutch oven over medium-high heat. When oil is very hot, add the pork and the remaining 1½ teaspoons salt. Cook, stirring often, until the pork is well browned and cooked through, about 15 minutes. Push the pork to one side of the pan and stir the masa into the fat; blend well. Stir in the cooked nopales and the chili puree. Add the cumin and oregano, stirring well. Simmer over low heat for 10 minutes. Adjust seasoning as needed, adding cayenne, if desired. Serve hot in soup bowls.

(Santos Silerio)

SQUARE PLATE BREAD PUDDING WITH CUSTARD SAUCE

Yield: 10 to 12 servings

5 eggs
4 cups milk
2 teaspoons ground cinnamon
1 cup raisins
1 pound day-old baguettes, torn into bite-size pieces
Brown sugar

Custard Sauce

¾ cup sugar
3 egg yolks, lightly beaten
⅛ teaspoon salt
¼ cup water
3 tablespoons butter, cut into small bits
2 tablespoons cornstarch
1½ cups boiling water
2 teaspoons clear vanilla extract

Preheat oven to 350 degrees. Grease a 9-by-13-inch glass baking dish and set aside. Combine the 5 eggs, milk, cinnamon, and raisins in a large bowl; whisk to blend well. Add the baguette pieces and stir to combine. Turn out mixture into prepared baking dish and bake in preheated oven for 45 minutes, or until top of pudding springs back when lightly pressed. Cool on rack.

While the pudding is baking, make the Custard Sauce. Cream the sugar and egg yolks in mixing bowl until mixture is fluffy and a pale lemon yellow in color. Add salt, ¼ cup water, and butter. Beat until well blended. Add the cornstarch and beat to blend. Slowly add the boiling water, while beating, until well combined. Turn mixture out into a heavy-bottomed saucepan and cook over medium heat until thickened, stirring constantly. Add vanilla extract and blend.

Cut pudding into squares and serve warm, topped with warm Custard Sauce.

(The Square Plate)

The Square Plate

Mason

For almost thirty years, Larry and Barbara Brown were the successful proprietors of Engel's Deli, a popular breakfast and lunch spot in Fredericksburg. After the last of their seven children graduated from high school, Larry and Barbara were ready for a rest. They sold the deli and spent a year in New Mexico. However, the couple realized that Texas was really home, so they headed back. ❦ Having been in the restaurant business for so long, they weren't satisfied with being idle. So they decided to establish a small eatery in Mason by remodeling a vintage building they owned on the town square. With her flair for creating spaces with ambiance, Barbara transformed the building into a cozy, small-town café with the original storefront windows and glass doors and with a nostalgic feel that brings back memories of an earlier time. The aromas of good coffee, desserts fresh from the oven, and simmering soups beckon patrons to have a seat and open up the newspaper. ❦ The Square Plate, open for lunch only, has a tempting array of sandwiches, such as Grilled Reuben on Rye, good old Egg Salad, and a toasted goat cheese, pesto, and tomato sandwich served on ciabatta bread. The full-meal salads include Fruited Chicken Salad, the most popular item at the Browns' deli in Fredericksburg. The menu also offers homemade soups that change daily as well as a schnitzel plate and a German sausage plate, served with either kraut or red cabbage. The sides are all lovingly prepared, and the potato salad is a delicious, unique concoction with a vinegar and oil dressing. A daily Hot Lunch Special consists of classics like meatloaf or other comfort foods that won't disappoint. An old-fashioned glass deli case is filled to the brim with such classics as carrot cake, bread pudding, cheesecake, brownies, chocolate pecan bourbon pie, caramel apple pie, and other goodies. ❦ With Larry in the kitchen and Barbara behind the counter, the Browns love what they're doing, and the evidence comes on square plates. You won't leave hungry.

212 Fort McKavitt • (325) 347-1911 • www.sqplate.com

Tallent Vineyard

Mason

Drew Tallent is a fourth-generation Mason County farmer who knows the responsibilities that come with stewardship of the family farm. He's a man with a remarkably serene temperament, very much in tune with nature and all its nuances. He's raised watermelons, peanuts, wheat, sesame, guar beans, cantaloupes—whatever crops would keep the farm profitable and in the family. ❦ When wine grapes began to make the Texas scene on a large scale, Drew researched the profitability of growing grapes and decided this crop might work for the farm. He planted four acres of cabernet sauvignon, and the vines flourished. The following year, he planted eighteen additional acres in syrah, malbec, and grenache. Drew had met Richard Becker, owner of Becker Vineyards, who had indicated a need for malbec in Texas. So Tallent Vineyard grew the grapes for Becker Vineyard's first Malbec, released in late spring of 2007 to great acclaim. Eventually Drew also planted pinot grigio, merlot, mourvèdre, and petit verdot varietals. ❦ He learned to fight the late-spring freezes so common in the area by installing one of the first sprinkler systems in the Hill Country to completely cover the vines with a layer of ice during the freeze. When the freeze is over, the ice melts and the tiny buds keep right on growing. In 2006, however, the

grapes couldn't survive the three vicious hailstorms that pounded the fields, also wiping out that year's peach and berry crops. ❦ With his dry sense of humor, Drew jokingly says, "You know how to make a small fortune in the grape-growing business? Start with a large one!" ❦ On any given day, you'll see Drew working somewhere on the farm. There's nothing easy about keeping tractors, sprayers, pumps, and drip systems working or making sure that all the pruning, hedging, and tucking is done on the vines and all the rows are mowed. It's a continuous process to make the finest grapes possible on the Hickory Sands of Mason County. ❦ The vineyard is not open to the public, but serious oenophiles may call to arrange a tour.

(325) 258-4489

Love Creek Orchards, The Apple Store and Patio Café

Medina

Baxter and Carol Adams, founders of Love Creek Orchards, are special folks who have given Texas a couple of real treasures. In 1981 they purchased 1,863 acres along Love Creek in the Bandera Canyonlands west of Medina. The land was totally depleted, but they fell in love with its rugged beauty and began to grow dwarf apple trees that produce regular-size fruit and ripen early. Their success gave rise to a flourishing apple-growing industry around Medina. In the mid-1990s they planted a second apple orchard in the town of Medina. They purchased a rock house in the middle of town where they could sell their apples, and soon the store was much more than just an apple market. They added local arts and crafts , jams and jellies, breads, sauces, butters, and their now legendary, washtub-size apple pies made from their Pink Lady apples. The Apple Store became a tourist destination, and soon the Adamses added the Patio Café. ❦ In 2007, as they approached retirement, they sold the store and its café to Bryan and Stacie Hutzler, who had always loved the store and worked hard to continue its great legacy. The Hutzlers still offer the same varieties of fresh apples and apple-based goodies, but they have expanded the Patio Café. Their work has paid off! In 2011 Texas Monthly named the Patio Café one of the "Best 40 Small-Town Cafes in Texas." Every nook and cranny of the store is filled with great gift items with an apple theme and you can purchase the dwarf apple trees grown by Baxter Adams. ❦

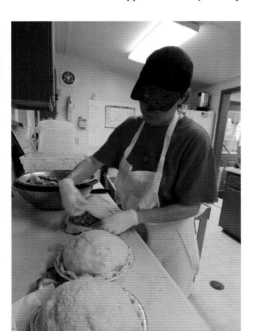

The Baxters continue to operate Love Creek Orchards right down the road, where you can still pick your own apples, blackberries, and peaches in season (visit the Web site for picking times). You can also purchase Big Leaf "Lost" Maple trees, which Baxter Adams brought back from the brink of extinction in Texas. The Adamses' second gift to Texas came about in 2000, when they sold 1,400 acres of their original Love Creek Ranch to the Nature Conservancy to create the Love Creek Preserve.

Love Creek Orchards • 13558 State Hwy. 16 North • (830) 589-2588 • www.lovecreeknursery.com

The Apple Store and Patio Café • 14024 State Hwy. 16 North • (830) 589-2202 • www.lovecreekorchards.com

APPLE BUTTERMILK LOAVES

Yield: 2 loaves

3 cups all-purpose flour
½ teaspoon baking powder
½ teaspoon baking soda
¼ teaspoon salt
½ pound (2 sticks) butter
1 cup granulated sugar
1 cup firmly packed brown sugar
3 eggs
1 teaspoon vanilla
¾ cup buttermilk
½ pound apples, peeled, cored, and finely chopped (1½ cups)
½ cup chopped pecans
1 teaspoon grated orange zest

Preheat oven to 350 degrees. Grease and flour two 8½-by-4½-by-2⅝-inch loaf pans; set aside. Combine the flour, baking powder, baking soda, and salt in a large bowl, tossing to blend well; set aside. In bowl of electric mixer, cream the butter, sugar, and brown sugar; beat in the eggs one at a time, scraping down the sides of the bowl after each addition. Add vanilla; beat just to blend. Add the buttermilk alternately with the flour mixture, scraping down the sides of the bowl after each addition. Add the apples, pecans, and orange zest. Beat just to blend. Divide the batter between the two prepared loaf pans. Bake for 50 to 60 minutes, or until a toothpick inserted near the center comes out clean. Cool in the pans for 10 minutes, then turn out loaves onto a wire rack and cool completely. Wrap and let stand overnight to allow flavors to blend.

(Love Creek Orchards)

STEWED SQUASH WITH SHRIMP AND SPINACH SOUP

Carol Taylor says that her partner Chef Mike Hennessey is perhaps best known for his Soup of the Day. "Who would have thought that West Texans would eat soup all year round?" she asked. "We certainly underestimated the simple practical comfort of a meal of homemade soup!" Carol says many people have driven quite a distance to get some of this soup.

Yield: 4 to 6 servings

¼ pound (1 stick) butter
1 large yellow onion, chopped
4 celery sticks, chopped
2½ pounds yellow squash, chopped
2 cups chicken broth
3 ounces fresh baby spinach, chopped fine
½ pound small (70–90 count) shrimp, peeled and deveined
½ teaspoon freshly ground white pepper
Salt to taste
1 cup whipping cream

Melt the butter in a heavy 3-quart saucepan over medium heat. Add the onion, celery, and squash. Sauté, stirring often, until the vegetables are wilted and very tender, about 20 minutes. Remove from heat and puree the vegetables in a blender until smooth. Return the puree to the pan and add all remaining ingredients. Stir to blend well and cook until the shrimp have turned a rich coral-pink color, about 15 minutes. Serve hot.

(Sideoats Café & Bakery)

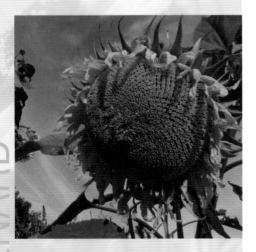

Sideoats Café & Bakery

Menard

When two of Menard's restaurants closed in 2002, the small town really felt the loss—especially the devoted bridge players who had lost their game venues. Carol Taylor decided that the community needed a gathering place with good, fresh, affordable food and set about to open one. Carol also figured that since Menard is the eastern gateway to the Great Plains, the restaurant would be a good stopping place for hungry travelers. ❀ Two years later, in 2004, Carol opened the Sideoats Café & Bakery. She named it for sideoats grama, which was designated the state grass of Texas in 1971. A nutritious, drought-tolerant grass that is highly prized by ranchers like Carol's husband, the grass seemed to be a fitting name for a café emphasizing good, nutritious food. ❀ Carol first met Chef Mike Hennessey when he was working for a well-know catering firm in San Angelo. She'd loved his food, and in 2005 they became partners in Sideoats. Mike describes himself as a "street chef"—completely self-taught. He's done a marvelous job of developing the "upscale down-home" menu, which offers a diverse selection of items, including a very worthy chicken-fried steak. Mike says his Grilled Flat Iron Steak, topped with a blue cheese–scallion butter, is becoming one of the most popular items on the menu. ❀ Sideoats is open for breakfast, lunch, and dinner. Lunch offers a variety of cold and grilled sandwiches served on house-baked LaBrea breads, delicious burgers, and Mike's great soups. The bakery makes fabulous cinnamon rolls and other breakfast pastries, muffins, and unique desserts. Fresh-baked LaBrea breads can be purchased by the loaf.

509 Ellis Street (U.S. 83) • (325) 396-2069 • www.sideoatscafe.com

Huisache Grill and Wine Bar

New Braunfels

Huisache Grill opened in 1994 in a building that had a long history as a restaurant site in historic downtown New Braunfels. Owners Don and Lynn Forres jokingly say that it "had more holes in its walls than wall, little street presence, and the charm of an active railroad track fifteen feet from the building." ❦ But through a remodeling and expansion project in 1998, Don and Lynn created a casual, unique restaurant offering moderately priced but inno-

vative lunches and dinners with an extensive beer and wine list. ❦ Each of the three dining areas resulting from the renovation and expansion has its own distinctive personality. The small front

dining room has a sleek, modern feel with soft coloring. The large dining room and bar area has a rustic feel with a high vaulted ceiling and exposed rustic beams. A rear dining room has a homey, country-café look. ❦ Huisache Grill boasts friendly, prompt, and caring service, plus great food. The menu has a wide and varied selection of salads, including the outstanding Asian Salmon Salad Plate, as well as soups, really innovative sandwiches, grilled steaks, seafood dishes, and other seafood items. The menu also features pork chops, pasta, chicken dishes, and a very good version of the Hill Country mainstay, chicken-fried steak. Desserts are all made in the restaurant kitchen and include a superb Italian Cream Cake.

303 W. San Antonio Street • (830) 620-9001 • www.huisache.com

SHRIMP AND CRAWFISH BISQUE

Yield: 12 servings as soup course,
6 servings as entrée

½ cup butter
¼ cup minced onions
¼ cup minced celery
½ cup flour
½ gallon milk
2 tablespoons chicken base
½ teaspoon ground white pepper
½ pound cooked cocktail shrimp
1 pound crawfish tails
2 cups dry sherry (not cooking sherry)

Melt the butter in a heavy 6-quart pot. Add the celery and onions and cook gently over low heat until translucent. Add the flour all at once and stir to blend well. Stir over low to medium heat to make a light, blond-colored roux. Slowly add the milk, then add the chicken base and white pepper. Cook for about 30 minutes, or until soup has thickened. Add shrimp and crawfish tails. Stir in sherry, blending well; cook for 5 minutes. Serve hot.

(Huisache Grill and Wine Bar)

GERMAN POTATO SOUP

This soup is a hands-down favorite at the New Braunfels Smokehouse. Through the years, it has warmed the souls of many weary travelers. The bits of dried beef add a rich, smoky taste.

Yield: 4 servings

3 tablespoons butter
½ cup chopped onion
4 large potatoes, peeled and cubed
2 teaspoons salt
1 teaspoon black pepper
7 cups water
3 ounces Smokehouse Dried Beef, shredded, or substitute 3 ounces cooked, chopped smoked bacon

Melt the butter in a heavy 6-quart soup pot. When butter has melted and the foam subsides, add the onions and sauté until wilted and transparent, about 5 minutes. Add the remaining ingredients except the dried beef. Bring to a boil, reduce heat, and simmer until potatoes are very soft, about 1 hour. Ladle the soup into bowls and top with the dried beef.

Variation: To make Vichyssoise, use 6 cups water and add 1 cup half-and-half and ¼ cup chopped chives to the recipe. Serve well chilled.

(New Braunfels Smokehouse)

New Braunfels Smokehouse

New Braunfels

The legendary New Braunfels Smokehouse started out as an ice plant where local farmers and ranchers brought their meats for cold storage. In 1943 San Antonio businessman and cattle rancher Russell Kemble "Kim" Dunbar bought the plant. Benno Schuenemann, the manager, had a talent for smoking meats and would use old German recipes to cure and smoke the customers' meats. His hickory-smoked hams, turkeys, and sausages were the talk of the entire area.
❊ As word spread, Kim Dunbar and his wife, Arabel, set up a mail-order business and then in 1952 opened a Tasting Room, inspired by old Smoky Mountain smokehouses with their bent stovepipes, leaning walls, and rustic furnishings. Thus the New Braunfels Smokehouse restaurant was born. ❊ In 1967, with the business growing, the original building was moved across the highway to its present location just off I-35 and expanded. The Yard, a shaded outdoor area that was opened in 1986, is the latest addition.
❊ The Dunbars' daughter and son-in-law, Susan and Dudley Snyder, now own and operate the New Braunfels Smokehouse. The restaurant serves breakfast, lunch, and dinner and is still a favorite stop with travelers. Its mail-order business, now expanded to include Internet sales, continues to grow.

1090 Business Hwy. 35• (830) 625-2416 • www.nbsmokehouse.com

Cool Mint Café

San Marcos

Cool Mint Café opened its doors in 2006 in a 1920s Arts and Crafts bungalow adjacent to the Texas State University campus and the San Marcos Historic District. ❄ The goal of chef and owner Suzanne Perkins is to serve fresh, high-quality ingredients in interesting combinations and with skillful preparation and presentation. "We want our guests to leave the table satisfied and feeling better after they eat rather than feeling stuffed and dull by getting little or no nutritional value from the meal," she says. ❄ Cool Mint Café uses fresh, local organic vegetables and poultry and only fresh herbs, which come from Suzanne's extensive herb gardens. ❄ Armed with a background of managing resorts on California's Monterey Peninsula, Suzanne serves the community with a full café menu, an in-house bakery, and a take-out market offering fast service. Cool Mint also does catering and special-events planning. ❄ Diners are greeted with a tray of hot Texas yeast rolls made from scratch in the café's bakery, as are all of the desserts. The menu is simple, yet fun, and loaded with nutritious and delicious goodies. Appetizers range from a savory Mexican Cheesecake to an excellent Greek Platter—hummus served with olives, roasted peppers, and cucumber slices with toasted pita wedges. The Tomato-Basil Bisque is served with a mini grilled-cheese sandwich; heartier dishes include grilled entrées served with fresh sauces or salsas. Desserts from the bakery offer a selection of unique flavor pairings. ❄ The café composts all vegetable trimmings, and Suzanne continually strives to use ecologically beneficial practices while producing the finest-tasting, most nutritional foods possible. She's accomplished that goal handily. You'll never suspect that those fabulous tastes on the plate are actually good for you!

415 Burleson Street • (512) 396-2665
• www.coolmintcafe.com

GARDEN GAZPACHO

Yield: 4 to 6 servings

6 medium tomatoes, seeded
2 medium cucumbers, peeled and seeded
Half of a large green bell pepper
Half of a large yellow bell pepper
1 medium sweet onion
¼ cup red wine vinegar
¼ cup extra-virgin olive oil
¼ cup Worcestershire sauce
2 tablespoons minced garlic chives
2 tablespoons minced fresh thyme
2 tablespoons minced fresh oregano
1 quart well-chilled tomato juice
2 cups ice cubes
Salt and pepper to taste
Additional chopped herbs for garnish
Lime slices for garnish

Chop the vegetables into medium dice. Combine in a large bowl and stir in the vinegar. Add olive oil, Worcestershire sauce, herbs, tomato juice, and ice cubes, blending well. Season with salt and pepper. Refrigerate until ready to serve. The ice will, of course, melt, so stir well just before serving. Garnish with additional herbs and a slice of lime per serving.

(Cool Mint Café)

G&R Grocery & Market

San Saba

San Saba is a charming small town at the northern boundary of the Hill Country. It's located adjacent to the San Saba River with its clear water and famous pecan bottoms. It's the county seat of San Saba County, so it's got a courthouse square with an array of shops and businesses. One of those shops in particular, right smack across the street from the courthouse, stands out. The G&R Grocery could have been lifted right out of Mayberry and plucked down there in San Saba. Except that the G&R Grocery has been around a lot longer than the TV Mayberry of my childhood. ❉ G&R Grocery was established over sixty-two years ago, in 1946. And Edward Ragsdale, who opened the market, is still its sole proprietor. It's the kind of store where I remember shopping as a kid with my grandparents on visits to their rural home. The well-worn wooden floors have a polished patina, and the original wooden bins and shelves hold canned goods and modern cleaning products. There are all the staples you need and a side room with charming old produce cases, perhaps the original ones, and, yep, still filled with fresh produce. ❉ The meats are fresh, arranged in an old meat case in the back of the store. I couldn't resist the temptation to purchase some of the best-looking pork chops I've seen in years. Thick-cut and rimmed with a half-inch ring of pork fat, just like the ones my mother used to fry up when we were kids, back in the good old days before we knew the evils that lurked in that delicious fat. I'd save the fat for the last and eat every bite of it! Where on earth did Mr. Ragsdale find those fat pigs? There were two-inch-thick rib eyes with incredible marbling and the biggest briskets I've ever seen. I tried to picture the truly awesome steers from

which they must've come. Sausages and thick-sliced bacon were arranged in neat rows, next to fat hens, rump roasts, and spare ribs. I was very much like a kid in a candy store standing there in front of all that beautiful meat! ❉ G&R Grocery was a divine discovery, a small-town treasure. If I lived in San Saba, I'd shop there. As it is, I have to make a long drive when I go back for more of that meat! ❉ Long live Edward Ragsdale and the G&R Grocery in San Saba, Texas!

502 E. Commerce Street • (325) 372-3364

The Great San Saba River Pecan Company

San Saba

San Saba is known as the Pecan Capital of Texas, and local folks take that designation seriously. So Larry and Martha Newkirk were elated when they had the opportunity to purchase an existing orchard of 10,000 pecan trees in 1988. Originally planted in 1968, the orchard had suffered from a few years of neglect, but the Newkirks slowly nourished the majestic trees back into shape for their commercial operation. ❧ The Great San Saba River Pecan Company is located in a beautiful parklike setting just west of town and bounded by four and a half miles of San Saba River frontage. It's a lovely place to visit, and the Newkirks have provided plenty of picnic tables where you can have a lovely picnic under the pecan trees. Martha's wall exhibit inside the charming retail shop tells the story of the area's pecan industry. ❧ The orchard is planted with the Western Schley variety, a very tasty paper-shell pecan and the most popular with commercial growers in the area. You can pick your own pecans during the season (November–January); old-fashioned cane poles are available for thrashing the pecans from the trees! Or you can purchase unshelled and shelled pecans by the pound at the retail shop or via the Web site. ❧ The shop also offers myriad pecan products made by the company, many packaged in attractive gift baskets. Your mouth will water at the free samples set up for you to taste around the store: fresh-brewed Pecan Coffee, various fruit and berry preserves combined with pecans, chocolate-covered pecans, and sweet and spicy seasoned pecans, or just plain, pristine pecan halves. Pecan Popcorn is a unique treat, and the Peach, Pecan & Amaretto Preserves won a coveted first prize in the Most Outstanding Preserve category at the International Fancy Food Show in New York. ❧ The Great San Saba River Pecan Company also produces baked goods: fruitcake, cinnamon-pecan streusel, pecan nut breads, and the award-winning Traditional Pecan Pie. One of the Newkirks' most unique products is Pecan Pie in a Jar—just pour the contents of the jar into a nine-inch pie shell, bake, and you've got yourself one fine pecan pie! ❧ All of the goodies produced by the company are made and shipped from facilities on the premises.

234 U.S. 190 West • (800) 621-9121 • www.greatpecans.com

TRADITIONAL PECAN PIE

Yield: One 9-inch pie

3 tablespoons butter
2 teaspoons vanilla extract
¾ cup sugar
3 eggs, well beaten
1 cup medium or large pecan pieces
1 cup light corn syrup
⅛ teaspoon salt
1 prepared unbaked 9-inch pie shell
½ cup pecan halves

Preheat oven to 450 degrees. Cream the butter and vanilla together, gradually adding the sugar. Add the eggs, beating well. Thoroughly blend in the pecan pieces, corn syrup, and salt. Turn the mixture out into the prepared pie shell. Bake in preheated oven for 10 minutes; reduce heat to 350 degrees, arrange the pecan halves over the top and bake an additional 30 to 35 minutes, or until the pie is set. Cool on wire rack before serving.

Note: Martha says you can make another excellent dessert—one with virtually no preparation—by using the Great San Saba River Pecan Company's Peach, Pecan & Amaretto Preserves: simply stir one jar of the preserves into a quart of softened vanilla ice cream, pour into a prepared graham cracker pie crust, and refreeze. Before serving, top with slices of fresh fruit and whipped cream.

(The Great San Saba River Pecan Company)

Oliver Pecan Company

San Saba

It was a late August afternoon when I first visited the 350-acre San Saba River "bottom" pecan orchard of the Oliver Pecan Company, known as its "home orchard." There was a certain earthy, slightly fecund smell to the land, rimmed by the meandering San Saba River, with the dense growth of towering native pecans overhead. On the ground there were patches of sunlight streaking through the trees. Wind rustled through the old branches, waving the heavy pecan clusters against a cerulean sky. ❦ Native Texas pecan trees were mentioned in Spanish explorer Cabeza de Vaca's report to the king of Spain in 1542. The tree has proven itself to be a survivor and is very resistant to drought, sending its taproot to astonishing depths to find water. The native pecan is tough nut to crack, however, with a very thick shell, making it a less attractive variety for commercial growers. But the intense flavor of the nut is preferred by fine bakeries. Native Texas pecans are the only pecans used by the Blue Bell Creamery in Brenham, makers of Blue Bell ice cream. ❦ Oliver Pecan Company began in 1970 when Gordon Lee and Clydene Oliver bought a piece of property on the San Saba River that had about 250 native pecan trees. To harvest the crop that fall, they used cane threshing poles and a lot of buckets. Eventually they established orchards with other varieties of pecan trees that are more commercially attractive than the native pecan. A few years later Gordon Lee was one of the first pecan growers in the Hill Country to use mechanical harvesting equipment. In 1980 they established a warehouse in Belmont to purchase pecans from other growers and broker them to major pecan-shelling companies. ❦ In 1984 the Olivers opened a warehouse and retail store in San Saba. Soon a shelling plant to process their own pecans followed, then a candy kitchen. Oliver Pecan makes over seventy-five different pecan-laden goodies in the candy kitchen. A warehouse was opened in San Angelo in 1992 to serve the West Texas growers, along with a custom shelling plant. ❦ Little did Gordon Lee and Clydene know that their 250 trees would be the beginning of a family pecan dynasty! Every child, spouse, and grandchild in the family is involved in the operation of the company in one capacity or another. The Olivers now have pecan orchards in San Saba, Gonzales, Luling, Belmont, Goldthwaite, and DeLeon, with a total of approximately 40,000 trees. Their operation also includes pecan retail stores in San Saba and San Angelo, a mail-order catalog, Web site, wholesale, and fundraising, in addition to a gourmet kitchen store in San Angelo (SugarBaker's), a gift shop in San Saba, a grain elevator, a fertilizer company, farming, and cattle. Gordon Lee passed away in 2000, but the company marches on under the direction of Clydene, sons Shawn and Mark, daughter Marcie Maxcey, and their spouses and children, all operating the family business.

1402 W. Wallace Street • (325) 372-5771 • www.oliverpecan.com

Sister Creek Vineyards

Sisterdale

Sister Creek Vineyards is located in the heart of the tiny Sisterdale community between the east and west forks of cypress-lined Sister Creek. Recently discovered historical documents indicate that vineyards were planted in this area in the 1860s. ❋ The winery, housed in a restored 1885 cotton gin, was established in 1988 by rancher Vernon Friesenhahn and his helper, Danny Hernandez, at a time when the rebirth of the Texas wine industry was in its infancy. Danny had gained an appreciation for wine in the 1970s while stationed in Germany, and the time-honored secrets that local winemakers shared with him proved to be beneficial when he became

the winemaker at Sister Creek Vineyards. Twenty years later, he's still handcrafting each bottle with gusto, passion, and great joy. ❋ Danny uses classic French (Bordeaux and Burgundy) winemaking techniques to produce the Sister Creek wines. He ages the wines in sixty-gallon oak barrels for up to three years and uses minimal filtration to allow the wines to retain their fullest flavors. ❋ Sister Creek produces Chardonnay, Pinot Noir, Merlot, and superb Cabernet Sauvignon blends. One of its most noteworthy wines, and an excellent dessert wine, is a Muscat Canelli Reserve, a well-balanced wine that has intense fruit and a rich, long finish. It's a fun wine to which Danny adds just a hint of carbonation, making it spritz around the palate.

1142 Sisterdale Road • (830) 324-6704 • www.sistercreekvineyards.com

THE POODIE BURGER

Poodie Locke was the master of Hill Country bar food—and what better bar food is there than a really bodacious burger? The Poodie Burger ranks at the top of the list of best burgers around. Hatch chilies are essential to the fabulous taste of the Poodie Burger. This variety of Anaheim chili is grown only around Hatch, New Mexico, and is available only from late August to early September. When you find them in the supermarket, buy up tons of them, blister and peel them, then freeze them in small quantities so you can make Poodie Burgers 'til next year's crop.

Yield: Six 6-ounce patties

2¼ pounds ground Black Angus chuck, 80/20 meat-to-fat ratio

Salt and freshly ground black pepper

6 slices Monterey Jack cheese

Buttered and toasted burger buns

Hatch Chili Blend (see recipe below)

Grilled Onions (see recipe below)

Mustard and mayonnaise

Sliced hamburger pickles

Chopped raw onions

Iceberg lettuce leaves

Hatch Chili Blend

3 tablespoons butter

6 Hatch chilies, blistered, peeled, seeded, and cut into ½-inch dice

1 small onion, chopped

3 large garlic cloves, minced

Grilled Onions

1 large onion, sliced about ⅜-inch thick

Canola oil

Poodie's Hilltop Bar and Grill

Spicewood

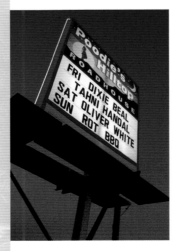

To the fans of great Texas music, fabulous bar food, camaraderie, boot scootin', and, yes, beer and other libations of a stronger nature, Poodie's Hilltop Bar and Grill is a Hill Country legend. Now this ain't one of those places that puts an *e* on the end of "grill." It's an unassuming-looking place, one that you'll likely miss in the hustle and bustle of the present-day Highway 71 area between Oak Hill and Spicewood if you're not really looking for it. But don't be misled by the rather unremarkable exterior. Opened in 1998 by Randall "Poodie" Locke, Poodie's has long been a haven for bikers, musicians and wannabes, rockers young and old, aging hippies, schoolteachers, and button-down types. Inside you'll find the usual bar paraphernalia, but take a closer look and you'll find personalized photos of country music giants covering every inch of space not covered by a neon beer sign. Music memorabilia clutters every available nook and cranny. Before his death in 2009, Poodie Locke was Willie Nelson's road manager, a "day job" that he held down for over thirty years. Oh, the stories Poodie could tell! Every now and again, Willie, who lives right down the road, might

just show up at Poodie's to throw back a brew or two and say howdy all around. The food at Poodie's is legendary in its own right. The Poodie Burger, with a side of hand-cut fries, is a masterpiece of decadently delicious, drip-down-the-front-of-your-shirt bar food. In addition to the comfort food, there's live music, dancing, pool, and shuffleboard—and a huge, two-level deck outside under the oak trees where you can watch a pretty special sunset. Imbued with Poodie's huge *joie de vivre*, the roadhouse continues to operate. If you squint, you just might catch his image at the end of the shuffleboard table.

22308 State Hwy. 71 West • (512) 264-0318 • www.poodies.net

Divide the ground chuck into six equal portions and pat into firm patties with no cracks or gaps. Season both sides with salt and a liberal amount of black pepper. Refrigerate until ready to grill.

Make the Hatch Chili Blend. Melt the butter in a heavy 10-inch skillet over medium-high heat. Add the chopped chilies, onion, and garlic. Cook, stirring, until onions are wilted, transparent, and lightly browned, about 7 minutes. Remove from heat and set aside; keep warm.

Grill the patties to the desired degree of doneness. Set patties to one side of the grill and top with a slice of cheese. Keep the patties on the grill just until the cheese begins to melt. While patties are grilling, liberally brush the sliced onions with canola oil and grill, turning only once, until the onions are slightly charred and limp. Remove from grill and set aside; keep warm.

To assemble the burgers, spread mustard on one side of each toasted bun and mayonnaise on the other side. Place a burger on the bottom half of each bun and top with a portion of Hatch Chili Blend. Add a slice or two of the Grilled Onions. Add pickle slices, chopped raw onions, and top with a couple of lettuce leaves. Add top bun and chow down!

(Poodie's Hilltop Bar and Grill)

Spicewood Vineyards

Spicewood

Spicewood Vineyards, one of the state's more established wineries, was founded by Edward and Madeleine Manigold in 1992 near Marble Falls. The winery was a retirement project for the Manigolds, following long careers in public education. Passionate about making wines, they both studied enology and viticulture at the University of California at Davis and at Grayson County College in Denison, Texas. So it was not by sheer luck that the winery became so successful, winning medals in every level of competition. In 2007 the Manigolds retired again, selling their Spicewood Vineyards to Austin attorney and businessman Ron Yates, his parents, and his sister. ❀ Ron became infatuated with Spanish wines in the spring of 1999, when he spent time in Spain, a life-changing experience. He wound up going back to Spain for the next four summers, returning only to finish law school. One night while he was enjoying some Spanish wine with his parents and sister, they decided to talk to Susan and Ed Auler, founders of Fall Creek Vineyards, about planting some grapes on the family ranch in Cherokee, Texas. (Ron's dad and Ed are cousins.) Shortly afterward, Ron learned that Spicewood Vineyards was for sale, and the family ventured out to talk with the Manigolds. They fell in love with the property, but just to be sure it was the right decision, Ron worked with the Manigolds during the 2007 harvest. He found that working at the vineyard made him happier than he'd ever been before. A deal was struck, and the Yates family was in the wine business, despite cousin Ed's advice not to jump in head first! ❀ The Yateses have added another fifteen acres of vines to bring the total winery acreage to thirty-two. Although they continue to produce some of the signature varietals that the Manigolds started with, they have shifted the winery's focus to mainly Spanish and Portuguese varietals like Tempranillo, Touriga, Albarino, Graciano, and Verdejo. They also produce fruit from Texas High Plains growers and Tempranillo, Roussanne, and Viognier from vineyards near Brownfield. The Yateses have totally remodeled the entire facility, from the below-ground barrel room to the tasting room, and added a spectacular 5,500-square-foot event facility in 2009.

1419 CR 409 • (830) 693-5328 • www.spicewoodvineyards.com

Becker Vineyards

Stonewall

Becker Vineyards, located three miles west of Stonewall, was established in 1992 by Richard and Bunny Becker. They planted thirty-six acres of French vinifera vines on a site where native mustang grapes had once grown. The original planting has been expanded to forty-two acres that produce eight varietals. ❄ A reproduction of a nine-teenth-century German stone barn houses the winery and tasting room. Produced with French methods, the wines are aged in oak in the largest underground wine cellar in Texas. With a fermenting capacity of 35,000 gallons, Becker Vineyards sells out of its wines every year. But the Beckers want to keep their operation small—they're interested in quality, not quantity. In the first half of 2007, the winery bottled 42,000 cases of wine representing twenty-two varietals! ❄ Becker wines have won innumerable medals and awards, and they've been served at the White House and at state functions on several occasions. New varietals continue to be produced. In 2007 Becker Vineyards released its first bottlings of Barbera and Malbec to rave reviews. ❄ The tasting room is an inviting space that has been furnished with an antique bar from San Antonio's Green Tree Saloon. The decor also features arts and crafts by local artisans displayed in antique pie safes and armoires from the surrounding area. ❄ Visitors touring the facility can stay in the rustic Homestead Bed and Breakfast, a renovated log cabin from 1890. Also on the grounds is the Lavender Haus Recep-tion Hall, which is available for special events. ❄ With three acres behind the winery planted in lavender, Becker Vineyards hosts a very popular Lavender Festival each May. ❄ Becker wines and various lavender products are available through the Web site.

464 Becker Farms Road • (830) 644-2681 • www. beckervineyards.com

PORT WINE PECANS

These delectable little morsels are the creation of Paul Gingrich, who worked in the tasting room at Becker Vineyards for several years. Paul says they can be added to your favorite salad with a balsamic vinaigrette, sprinkled on ice cream, scattered over chocolate cake or cheesecake, crumbled over a warm wedge of Brie, or just munched like popcorn.

Yield: 2 cups

1 cup sugar
½ cup Becker Vineyards Vintage Port wine
2 cups pecan halves

Grease a heavy-duty baking sheet with solid shortening and set aside. Combine the sugar and wine in a heavy 14-inch skillet over medium-high heat. Stir the mixture constantly. When the sugar has dissolved and the syrupy mixture begins to boil, quickly stir in the pecans. Continue to stir, turning the pecan halves to prevent burning. Cook for about 5 to 6 minutes, or until the mixture has thickened and the syrup has turned a deep caramel color. Remove pan from heat and turn the pecans out onto the prepared baking sheet. Quickly separate the pecans into a single layer with a wooden spoon. (Take care not to touch the pecans; they are hot as blazes!) Allow pecans to cool for about 30 minutes, or until they are totally hardened. Store in a moisture-proof container.

(Paul Gingrich)

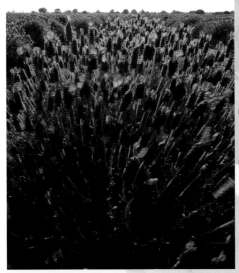

STONEWALL

ANCHO CHILI AND HONEY–BASTED QUAIL

Yield: 6 servings

12 semi-boneless quail
1 ancho chili, seeded and soaked in 1 cup of hot
    water for 30 minutes
1 garlic clove, peeled
2 tablespoons honey
1 teaspoon kosher salt

In a blender combine the ancho chili and soaking liquid, garlic, honey, and salt; puree until smooth.

Heat a gas grill to hot. Place the quail, breast side down, on the hot grill and cook for 3 to 4 minutes, or until skin is crisp. Turn over and baste with the ancho chili sauce. Cook for an additional 3 to 4 minutes. Move quail to cooler part of grill, turning them over so breast side is down and baste again. Keep turning and basting for 2 minutes more. Serve hot, basting again with the sauce.

(Mac & Ernie's Roadside Eatery)

Mac & Ernie's Roadside Eatery

Tarpley

Mac & Ernie's Roadside Eatery in Tarpley is a rare find. An even rarer find is the owner, Naylene Stolzer. ❀ Naylene started her culinary career at fifteen, when she got a job flipping burgers in her hometown of Boerne. Along life's road, she worked in various restaurants and learned the art of baking along the way. ❀ After Naylene married, she and her husband, Steve, started raising goats, as did their neighbors, the McKinnerneys. To market the goat meat, the McKinnerneys suggested opening a small restaurant (and thus inspired its name). ❀ They bought a portable building, a five-burner gas grill, a roaster oven, and a used refrigerator, then set up shop in the parking lot of Williams Creek Depot in 1999. Naylene did the cooking outdoors under a tin roof, and patrons ate at picnic tables scattered around the fringes of the parking lot. The menu consisted of cabrito tacos, fajitas, sausage wraps, and beans. ❀ The place was an instant hit, so the couples bought a deep fryer and added fried catfish to the menu—and later on, gourmet lamb, salmon, and quail dishes. Naylene added steaks as soon as she could afford steak knives. ❀ Mac & Ernie's Roadside Eatery was soon featured in *Texas Monthly*, *Southern Living*, and on the Food Network and the Travel Channel. Naylene's Cabrito Burger became legendary, and business boomed. ❀ In 2009 the Stolzers, now the sole owners, moved the eatery to a new location in Tarpley, complete with an indoor kitchen and dining room. The ambiance, however, was not lost. The portable building that once housed the whole restaurant is attached to the front of the new building to serve as a multipurpose entryway to the order counter. Order slips are passed to the kitchen via a ceramic goat that bleats, a system devised by Naylene's father. With the move, Naylene hired a couple of line cooks and expanded the menu again, although it still changes often. ❀ Mac & Ernie's is open for lunch and dinner on Fridays and Saturdays, for breakfast and lunch on Sundays. The breakfast menu includes strawberry-orange pancakes, spinach and goat cheese omelets, bacon waffles, and Naylene's outrageous version of Eggs Benedict. ❀ You still get your meal on a disposable plate with plastic utensils (except for the steak knives), but now you can enjoy a bottle of Silver Oak cabernet with your meal.

**11804 FM 470 • (830) 562-3727 •
www.macandernies.com**

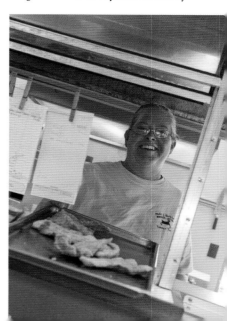

TARPLEY

Fall Creek Vineyards

Tow

Located on the northwest shore of beautiful Lake Buchanan and a few miles north of the tiny hamlet of Tow, Fall Creek Vineyards is one of the most picturesque of the Hill Country wineries. It is situated on the Fall Creek Ranch, owned by Ed Auler's family for five generations. Fall Creek is one of the pioneer Texas wineries and the very first in the Hill Country. ❄ The winery began in 1975 as an ambitious project of Ed and his wife, Susan, to determine whether high-quality wine grapes could be grown on their ranch. The Aulers' curiosity for the project was sparked during a trip to the wine-growing regions of France, where they had intended to study cattle operations. They noticed that the soil, terrain, and microclimate of their ranch were remarkably similar to those in

France. When they made the decision to give grape growing a try, they asked one of California's greatest winemakers, Andre Tchelistcheff, to come to Texas and have a look at their dirt. Andre determined that Fall Creek could grow notable red wine grape varietals from the Bordeaux region. After tasting their first bottling from the Aulers' experimental vineyards, Tchelistcheff wrote to them with the admonition "Plant more!" ❄ The present winery facility was opened in the spring of 1983, surrounded by a sea

of Texas bluebonnets. The ensuing years have seen the winery grow dramatically in size, quality, production, and recognition—Fall Creek has received too many accolades to list. ❄ Over the years the Aulers have maintained their cattle operations at the ranch while developing award-winning wines. They founded the legendary Texas Hill Country Wine & Food Festival, hosting its first event in April of 1986. They have also been active in lobbying for state legislation instrumental to the success of the Texas wine industry. ❄ In 1990 the Aulers opened their present tasting room, an elegant facility with an inviting courtyard. It's a great place to sip some of the good wines available in the tasting room and enjoy the Hill Country. ❄ Fall Creek produces many varietals, including the super-premium wine Meritus, a blend of cabernet sauvignon, merlot, and malbec, first introduced in 1998. One of Fall Creek's best-selling wines is Caché, a blend of six white grapes that closely resembles the flavor of California's popular Caymus Conundrum. ❄ Chad Auler, Ed and Susan's son, has recently assumed the winery's sales and marketing operation, taking Fall Creek Vineyards into its second generation as a family business.

1820 CR 2241 • (325) 379-5361 • www.fcv.com

Certenberg Vineyard

Voca

As a young boy, Houston native Alphonse Dotson was fascinated by a massive grape arbor at his grandfather's house. He'd watch the grapes grow every year—big clusters of them hanging everywhere. For forty years Alphonse never forgot those grapes, even though he went on to become a star football player and eventually wound up as a defensive linebacker for the Oakland Raiders. ❉ He lived for some ten years in Acapulco, where he had met his wife, Martha, but in the early 1990s the pair decided to move to the United States. Then Alphonse remembered those grapes again. ❉ After talking to winemakers and viticulture experts in both California and Texas, Alphonse was hooked on the idea of growing grapes. He made dozens of charts, researched the subject to death, and finally went looking for land. He and Martha settled on a parcel in McCullough County with the red, sandy soil that he had been looking for. ❉ Alphonse named the vineyard after that grape-growing grandfather, Alphonse Certenberg. The Dotsons planted thirty acres in chardonnay, cabernet sauvignon, merlot, and muscat canelli grapes in 1997. The opera-

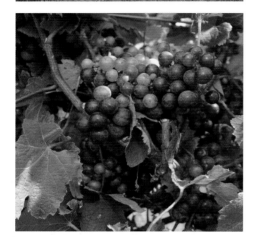

tion was totally hands-on at first because they simply weren't able to find help, but their hand-nurturing paid off in vigorous, healthy vines that produce high-quality wine grapes. ❉ Today Alphonse is affectionately referred to by fellow grape growers and winemakers as the state's "Celebrity Grape Grower." He was included on *Saveur* magazine's list of 100 Favorite Foods, Restaurants, Drinks, People, Places and Things. He served as the 2007–2008 president of the Texas Wine and Grape Growers Association. ❉ The Dotsons' dream is to open a small, very personal winery. ❉ The vineyard is not open to the public, but serious oenophiles may call to arrange a tour.

(325) 239-5500

VOCA

Welfare Café & Biergarten

Welfare

The community of Welfare, situated between Waring and Boerne in west-central Kendall County and accessible by only a small county road, declined in population for most of the past century. The store and post office closed in 1978 and remained abandoned until 1998, when Gabriele Meissner McCormick and David Lawhorn opened the Welfare Café in the building. ❧ They've left the building much the way it was, and it's that rustic feel which adds to the ambiance of the place. There's outdoor dining in relaxing spaces in the back overlooking the scenic grounds. The Goat Barn, newly constructed by David from vintage materials, is a fabulous space for private parties. It feels like stepping back in time, perhaps to a dining and dance hall of the 1800s. ❧ But the draw that has made the Welfare Café a destination eatery for residents from all

over the Hill Country and San Antonio is Gabrielle's food. The menu is a delightful, eclectic collection of very authentic German dishes, such as Rouladen (a stuffed filet of beef) and a selection of six different schnitzels, in addition to steaks and seafood. ❧ The wine list presents a nifty little collection of excellent labels and, of course, a lineup of great beers to enjoy in the Biergarten. Welfare Café is not a place where you stop for dinner on your way to the evening's entertainment—it is the evening's entertainment. The café is also open for lunch on Sundays.

233 Waring-Welfare Road • (830) 537-3700 • www.welfaretexas.com

CHICKEN FREDERICKSBURG

Chicken Fredericksburg is one of the most popular items on Gabrielle's menu, and she has graciously shared the recipe for the many fans of the dish.

Yield: 2 servings

- 2 tablespoons olive or canola oil
- 2 boneless, skinless chicken breasts, lightly floured
- 1 teaspoon minced garlic
- 1 teaspoon minced jalapeño, or to taste
- ¼ cup caramelized onions
- 1 ripe peach, peeled and sliced, with its juice
- 2 tablespoons dry white wine
- ½ cup whipping cream
- 1 tablespoon toasted pecan pieces

Spaetzle

- 2 eggs, beaten
- ½ cup milk
- 1½ cups all-purpose flour
- ¼ teaspoon salt
- ⅛ teaspoon freshly grated nutmeg
- 2 tablespoons butter

To make the spaetzle, combine the eggs and milk, then stir in flour, salt, and nutmeg, stirring until very smooth. Press the dough through a spaetzle maker or colander into boiling water. Boil for 2 to 3 minutes, then drain and set aside.

Prepare the chicken. Heat the oil in a heavy 10-inch skillet over medium heat. When oil is hot, sauté the chicken breasts on both sides until golden brown. Remove from pan, set aside, and keep warm. Add the garlic and jalapeño to the pan and cook until garlic is light tan. (Don't allow it to brown.) Add the onions and peach with its juice. Add the wine and deglaze the pan, scraping up browned bits from the bottom. Add the whipping cream. Return the chicken breasts to the pan and simmer until the sauce thickens, about 4 to 6 minutes.

While the sauce is thickening, finish cooking the spaetzle. Melt the butter in a heavy 10-inch skillet and sauté the spaetzle until light golden brown on the edges, about 3 to 4 minutes.

To serve, divide the spaetzle between two serving plates. Place a chicken breast on the spaetzle, top with a portion of the sauce, and garnish with toasted pecan pieces.

(Welfare Café & Biergarten)

WELFARE

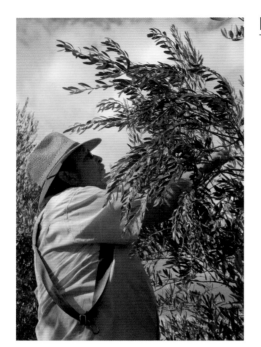

Bella Vista Ranch

Wimberley

Olives in the Texas Hill Country may sound like a pipe dream, but the concept was actually the real dream of Jack Dougherty and his wife, Patricia. Modeled on the traditional Italian family farm, the property, a former goat farm, has over 1,000 producing olive trees. The main varieties are Mission and Coratina, with the Barouni and Pendolino varieties planted for pollination. The Doughertys have recently planted Arbequina, a popular Spanish variety. They also grow blackberries, raspberries, figs, and tomatoes. ❀ Marketing their olive oil under the Alfresco brand and their operation as the First Texas Olive Oil Company, the Doughertys use an authentic, Italian-made *frantoio* (olive press) designed to extract a high volume of oil by the cold-press method. The fall of 2001 saw the first crop, and production has increased each year. ❀ The ranch's tasting room offers tastings of Alfresco Extra Virgin Olive Oil along with wines produced from the grapes and berries grown in the vineyards. The estate-bottled olive oil, wines, vinegars, olive-oil products, jams and jellies, books, soaps, and olive trees are available for purchase at the tasting room and through the online gift shop. ❀ The Doughertys conduct tours of the orchard, and during the harvest season (usually September and October) you can even participate in the picking and pressing process that goes into the making of fine olive oil.

3101 Mount Sharp Road • (512) 847-6514 • www.texasoliveoil.com

WIMBERLEY

Kiss the Cook Kitchen Essentials

Wimberley and Boerne

After owning a cookware store in the West Texas town of Abilene, partners and best friends Janet Galloway and Bren Kirschbaum relocated to Wimberley and opened Kiss the Cook in a little building on the downtown square in 2001. The pair opened a second store in Boerne in 2006 in a renovated old house right off Main Street in the quaint downtown shopping district. ❀ Both stores are stocked to the ceiling with a vast selection of kitchen gear that makes a serious cook's heart race. Customers from far and wide love shopping for the very finest cookware, kitchen gadgets, bakeware, small appliances, cutlery, linens, serving pieces—you name it. If it belongs in a kitchen, Bren and Janet have it! Furthermore, they can tell you how to use it. Hospitality and customer service are their top priorities. This philosophy has paid off, garnering Kiss the Cook recognition from *Southern Living* as a Southern Living Favorite in 2003 and one of the magazine's Fifty Top Shops in 2006. ❀ In the fall of 2007 the ambitious pair realized

their ultimate dream of opening a cooking school in a lovely new facility adjacent to the Boerne store. The classroom is equipped with the most up-to-date appliances and stocked with the fine cookware and gadgets available in the stores. Cookbook authors and chefs taught the first series of classes, which were eagerly attended and often produced waiting lists. ❀ The shop's Web site is a great resource for cooks, with all sorts of cooking tips and information, tons of recipes, and the opportunity to sign up for the newsletter. If you're a serious cook, then you'll want to make Kiss the Cook a destination stop.

**201 Wimberley Square (Wimberley) •
(512) 847-1553**

**113 E. Theissen Street (Boerne) •
(830) 249-3637 • www.kissthecooktx.com**

ROASTED POBLANO AND CORN CRAB CAKES WITH CHAYOTE SLAW

Yield: 6 to 8 servings

2 ears of fresh corn, shucked, or ½ cup frozen whole-kernel corn, thawed

1 tablespoon olive oil

1 red onion, cut into ¼-inch dice

2 garlic cloves, minced

1 poblano chili, blistered, peeled, and cut into ¼-inch dice

1 red bell pepper, blistered, peeled, and cut into ¼-inch dice

½ teaspoon ground cumin

1½ teaspoons chili powder

¼ teaspoon cayenne pepper

1½ teaspoons salt

¾ cup real mayonnaise

2 eggs, well beaten

1 cup panko bread crumbs, plus additional for breading

1 pound Gulf claw crabmeat

1 pound Gulf jumbo lump crabmeat

Canola oil

Chayote Slaw

2 chayote squash, cut into julienne strips

3 cups thinly sliced red cabbage

Juice of 1 lime

1 garlic clove, minced

1 cup real mayonnaise

½ cup buttermilk

¼ cup minced cilantro

½ jalapeño, seeded and minced

Salt and pepper to taste

Make the Chayote Slaw. Combine the chayote and cabbage in a large bowl; set aside. Combine the remaining slaw ingredients in a separate bowl and whisk to blend well. Pour the dressing over the reserved slaw and toss to blend well. Refrigerate while preparing the crab cakes.

Lightly oil the ears of corn and grill on a gas grill until golden brown, turning often. Allow to cool. Scrape the kernels from the cobs using a sharp knife; set aside. Heat the olive oil in a heavy-bottomed 12-inch skillet over medium heat. When the oil is hot, sauté the onion until limp and translucent, about 3 to 5 minutes. Add the garlic and sauté for 1 minute. (If you are using the frozen corn kernels, add them at this time.) Turn

(continued)

The Leaning Pear—Hill Country–Inspired Cuisine

Wimberley

The Leaning Pear, which opened in 2007 in the renovated Lowery House, one of the oldest structures in the area, brought to Wimberley a style of cuisine that could be summed up as "upscale down-home." ❋ Behind its success and the extraordinary cuisine are Matthew and Rachel Buchanan. The couple met while studying in Italy, and the Italian cuisine sparked Matthew's interest in cooking. He loved the passion that went into preparing the dishes, the slow cooking methods, and especially the fresh ingredients. When the pair returned to the states, Matthew attended the Culinary Institute of America in Hyde Park, New York, honing his skills and developing an eye for the best ingredients available. When he graduated, the couple decided

to open a restaurant in the Lowery House, part of a twelve-acre tract that Rachel's father had purchased. ❋ It took them five months to complete the renovation, which included equipping the postage-stamp-size kitchen. From the beginning Matthew has sourced his ingredients from local farmers, many of whom also grow specific crops for the restaurant. In the tiny kitchen Matthew and his staff prepare all of the stocks used in the soups and sauces. Everything is made from scratch, including the innovative desserts, so the menu reflects the seasonality of ingredients. The restaurant is also open on Sundays, when the dishes are predominantly brunch-oriented. Although the Sunday menu changes each week, the popular migas and quiches are mainstays. The daily soups and specials are inspired by whatever is available from fresh sources. In the spring Matthew takes advantage of fresh, local berries and peaches, using them in a variety of dishes. He also prepares locally produced meats, including fresh bison from Austin's Thunderheart Bison. ❋ The Buchanans have known for some time that the restaurant has simply outgrown the Lowery House. They plan to construct a new facility on the same property and with the same charm; this will allow them to expand the menu with grilled items and other dishes. The Lowery House will be turned into a marketplace offering takeout specials and locally grown and produced foods.

111 River Road • (512) 847-7327 • www.leaningpear.com

the onion mixture out into a large bowl. Add the blistered chilies, seasonings, mayonnaise, and beaten eggs. Stir to blend well. Stir in the bread crumbs and let the mixture stand for 1 minute. It should just barely hold together. If necessary add more bread crumbs. If the mixture is too stiff, add a bit more mayonnaise. Gently fold in the claw crabmeat, followed by the lump crabmeat, taking care not to break up the pieces. With your hands gently form baseball-size balls, flattening them into cakes. Roll each cake in the additional bread crumbs. The crab cakes can be refrigerated at this point for up to a day. Preheat oven to 400 degrees.

To cook the cakes, heat ½ inch of the canola oil in a heavy-bottomed 12-inch skillet over medium heat. When the oil is hot, add the crab cakes in a single layer and fry just until brown, turning once. Place the seared cakes on a wire rack set over a baking sheet and bake in preheated oven for 10 minutes.

To serve, place a portion of the Chayote Slaw in the center of each plate and top with a crab cake. Serve at once.

(The Leaning Pear)

Texas Specialty Cut Flowers
Wimberley

The bounty of gorgeous cut-flower arrangements from the Arnosky Family Farm has been providing bursts of welcome color and greenery to Hill Country homes since 1990. It's been a hard labor of love. ❀ On the farm's original twelve acres Frank and Pamela Arnosky built the first greenhouse and their bright blue home. When this acreage was in operation, they bought the adjoining eighteen acres. In 2003 they bought another one hundred acres on the site of the old Payton Colony, established in the 1870s as a free slave community. The former residents were tomato growers who took their tomatoes by mule cart to the tomato packing sheds at nearby Henly. The Arnoskys were able to buy the land only on the condition that they would continue to farm it. ❀ Today the Arnosky Family Farm has over forty acres in cultivation and fourteen greenhouses. In 2006, with the help of over 200 volunteers, the Arnoskys held an old-fashioned barn-raising at the Payton Colony site. Dubbed the Big Blue Barn, the structure houses the Farm Market, where you can purchase fresh-cut flowers, Pamela's gorgeous handmade bouquets, fresh-picked vegetables, locally made cheeses, fresh herbs, and plants. More than sixty kinds of flowers grown by Texas Specialty Cut Flowers are also sold at Central Market, Whole Foods Market, and select H-E-B stores in Texas as well as Farm to Market Grocery in Austin, King Feed in Wimberley, and McCall Creek Farms Mar-

ket in Blanco. ❀ The farm is truly a family operation, with each of the four Arnosky children having specific chores along with raising chickens, milk goats, rabbits, and horses. The Arnoskys believe in environmentally sound farming practices, using only organic compost as fertilizer, and are dedicated to supporting the return of the small family farm.

13977 FM 2325 • (830) 833-5428 •
www.texascolor.com

Wimberley Pie Company
Wimberley

Neal Mallard, the owner of Wimberley's beloved Wimberley Pie Company, is a very serious guy. That's probably why he's such a successful baker, even though it was a craft he learned somewhat late in life. Neal, a music major in college and still a passionate music lover, plays the trombone in several local groups and is also a ringer in the handbell choir at his church. Even his hobbies sound like a full-time job, but there's more . . . . ❄ Neal knew nothing about baking in 1989 when he bought the business, a wholesale operation that baked pies and cheesecakes for restaurants. But he jumped right in and learned the ropes—from Hobart mixers to Blodgett pizza ovens, where he bakes seventy-eight pies at a time! Neal does all the baking himself and has only one full-time employee. ❄ Wimberley Pie Company is now strictly retail and ships pies all over the country through phone orders in addition to operating a storefront where pies can be bought whole or enjoyed in the small dining room by the slice. The company now does as much business in November and December as it did in an entire year when Neal bought it. ❄ You won't believe the amazing array of pies available— from the ever-popular Apple and Cherry to seasonal favorites like Pumpkin to more unusual creations like Fudge Pecan and Peanut Butter. He even has pies we don't often see in the Hill Country—like Rhubarb-Strawberry. Cheesecakes, quiches, and cookies are also available ❄ Serious pies from a serious guy!

13619 RR 12 • (512) 847-9462 • www.wimberleypie.com

KEY LIME PIE

Yield: One 10-inch pie

Crust
1¼ cups finely ground graham cracker crumbs

2 tablespoons plus 1½ teaspoons granulated sugar

¼ cup melted butter

Filling
3 egg yolks

8 ounces cream cheese at room temperature

1 (14-ounce) can sweetened condensed milk

½ cup fresh lime juice or key lime juice

Sweetened whipped cream for garnish, if desired

Preheat oven to 350 degrees. Mix the graham cracker crumbs and sugar together, tossing to blend. Stir in the melted butter, coating well. Turn the mixture out into a 10-inch pie pan. Using the back of a spoon, press mixture against the sides of the pan to a thickness of ¼ inch, taking care to follow the slope of the pan. Spread the remaining mixture in the bottom of the pan and press down with a flat surface like the bottom of a measuring cup. Bake in preheated oven for 10 minutes. Remove from oven and allow to cool. (The crust can also be frozen for later use.)

While the crust is cooling, make the filling. Place the egg yolks in bowl of electric stand mixer and beat until light lemon yellow in color and very thick and "ribbonlike" in texture, about 5 minutes. Using a rubber spatula, scrape the thickened yolks into a separate bowl and set aside. Put the cream cheese in the mixer bowl and beat at medium speed until light and fluffy, scraping down the sides of the bowl often.

Return the yolks to the mixer bowl and beat at high speed for 3 minutes, scraping the sides of the bowl as needed. Add the sweetened condensed milk and mix at high speed for 3 minutes, scraping the bowl as needed. Add the lime juice and beat at medium speed for 3 minutes, scraping the bowl as needed. The mixture should begin to thicken slightly as you beat in the lime juice.

Pour the filling into the cooled pie crust and bake in 350 degree oven for 7 minutes. Allow the pie to rest for 30 minutes at room temperature, then place in an airtight container or carefully wrap in plastic wrap and refrigerate overnight before slicing. (This pie freezes quite well.)

Before serving, top each slice with a generous dollop of sweetened whipped cream, if desired.

(Wimberley Pie Company)

Acknowledgments

With each book project it always seems so difficult to know where to start in thanking all of the many people who helped to make it happen.

First, of course, there are the folks who are featured in this book. They generously arranged, and often rearranged, their schedules to accommodate our long itinerary, which was so often interrupted by the record rains of the spring and summer of 2007. Then there were my many e-mails and phone calls requesting clarification or just one more quote. I hope we've done you all the justice you so richly deserve for your contributions toward making the Texas Hill Country such a special place.

It was such an immense joy to work with my sister Sandy Wilson, photographer extraordinaire, for the first time on a book. Her stunning photos bring my words to life, allowing the reader to identify with the people and really see and feel all of the bounty of the Texas Hill Country featured in this book.

Many thanks are in order to my publisher, Kathy Shearer, for giving me the opportunity to do this book, especially knowing it's one she's wanted to publish for a long time. Kudos to Alison Tartt for her unparalleled editing skills, to Barbara Jezek for yet another superb job of book design, and to the entire team at Shearer Publishing for their hard work behind the scenes.

My dear bear of a husband, Roger, survived yet another book, lending his unfailing support as dinner cook, foot massager, and bedtime collaborator as I would read segments of the manuscript aloud in bed as I edited. His critiques and comments would often provide just the perfect phrase for which I was racking my brain.

And, as always, a profound thank you to those professional friends and mentors who helped me become who and what I am professionally—Nathalie Dupree, Shirley Corriher, Paul Prudhomme, Francois Dionot, Blake Swihart, Rose Beranbaum, and three who have left us: Lee Barnes, Bert Greene, and Sharon Tyler-Herbst.

Terry Thompson-Anderson
Fredericksburg, February 2008

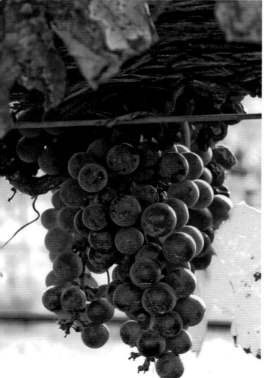

A book like this cannot be undertaken without the support and interest of more people than I can imagine, and I am extremely grateful to each of them. Of course, there is my sister and author Terry Thompson-Anderson and publisher Kathy Shearer, without whom I would never have had the opportunity to share in all these experiences. There is Barbara Jezek as well, the designer with whom I have worked over many years and whose book design can enhance any photographs.

My sister was unrelenting in her research of a complex assortment of people and places. She managed to schedule access to restaurants, kitchens, farms, retail shops, breweries, wineries, and people, all of whom were very generous with their time, throughout a large geographical area with the least amount of driving possible. And I cannot forget Roger Anderson, Terry's husband, who often had dinner on the table when we arrived, exhausted after a long day of driving, photographing, and interviewing.

I am very grateful to my friend Rosemary Schouten for educating me about both food and wine and their connection with the soil and people, without which I would have been unable to appreciate all the tasty things, beautiful places, and fascinating people I was photographing.

A very special thank you goes to my husband, Steve Freeman, who not only endured my prolonged absences but flew me back and forth in his plane several times for "just one more photo" in order to save me long hours on the road.

Sandy Wilson
Bellaire, February 2008

Index